CHAKRAS
FOR WITCHES

A Beginner's Guide to the Magic of the Body, Energy Healing, and Creating a Balanced Life

LISA CHAMBERLAIN
& LEANDRA WITCHWOOD

SPELLWORK AND SHADOWS

At one point or another, we all have issues that seem to defy our best magical efforts. No matter how much we *want* to believe that the results of a spell will come, we find that we still have some aspect of resistance, or doubt, that we can't shake.

This can be due to cultural conditioning, especially for aspiring witches—after all, we live in a society that doesn't recognize the validity of magic in the first place. But when something we want to change stays stubbornly in place no matter what we do, it's usually related to negative beliefs formed from our past experiences, which we may or may not be consciously aware of.

For example, lack of success in love magic can be caused by unconscious fears around being rejected or abandoned by a partner, or an inability to love and accept ourselves as we are. Money and abundance spells can be thwarted by feelings of unworthiness, or conflicting attitudes about money.

We may desire money for perfectly legitimate reasons (like paying the bills and having enough to eat), yet still experiencing this messy adventure we call "life on Earth." We simply have more knowledge and tools at our disposal for creating the best lives we can.

Many people believe that we attract circumstances and situations that our souls need to learn from in this incarnation. The witch with the regular job (which is most witches, by the way!) may be on Earth at this time to learn more about cooperating with others, rather than to win the lottery or live on a yacht. Or she may have unique gifts and skills that are meant to be used in service to the community. The psychic with the unfaithful spouse may be working through a karmic lesson in betrayal, which couldn't be experienced if he'd had a "heads up" in advance.

In the case of chronic illness, this is often (and some would argue *always*) an invitation to recognize and make peace with hidden aspects of ourselves that we've been denying, so we can heal and move on. All three of these situations are avenues for soul growth, whether we're witches or not, and regardless of our interest in or skill at magic.

Soul lessons notwithstanding, however, when magical workings are not successful, the underlying reason is always the same: the practitioner isn't in energetic alignment with the intention of the work. Some aspect of the psyche is in doubt, which prevents the manifestation from materializing on the physical plane. And no matter how well-timed your spell is, how long you charged your ingredients, or how brilliant your incantations may be, if the *belief* isn't there, the results won't be, either.

PROLOGUE: MAGIC AND THE BODY

When I was younger and brand-new to witchcraft and magic, I would read books about the Craft and wonder why their authors weren't multimillionaires, enjoying perfect health and wonderful relationships while living happily ever after.

How could a witch with decades of experience in spellwork still be financially dependent on a regular, non-magical full-time job? Were they just not very good at abundance and prosperity magic? If a witch develops a chronic illness, is it because they neglected to do a crucial healing or protection spell at some pivotal point in life? What about a highly psychic witch who learns that their spouse has been having an affair for the last six months? Did their psychic ability just disappear during that time?

Questions like these are reasonable to ask when we're trying to make logical sense out of magic and its effects on our lives. But it's helpful to remember that witches are not all-powerful, nor are we immune from life's headaches and heartbreaks. We are humans just like everybody else,

Editing and contributing to this book has inspired me to learn even more about the energy systems of the body, and possibly even study a form of energy healing for myself. Hopefully, reading it will inspire you to take the next step of your own journey—toward better health, a more balanced life, more ease and joy, and more powerful magic.

— Lisa Chamberlain, Editor and Co-author

While I've had a passing interest in the chakras before, my recent healing journey got me interested in focusing more on the "physical" aspects of the metaphysical realm. After all, witchcraft is essentially a means of integrating the energetic realm with the physical reality we find ourselves in, and the body is the very core of our physical reality. What better avenue to explore this magic through than the chakra system, which functions in both the physical and non-physical realms?

Leandra Witchwood is the perfect person to collaborate with on such an adventure. Not only is she an experienced witch, but she's also a certified Reiki master and a master herbalist. Leandra combines her knowledge and experience in a unique approach to healing through chakra work, mindfulness, magical tea rituals, and more, as you will see throughout this book.

She provides a beginner-friendly overview of the seven-chakra system and its role in managing the life-force energy that flows through the human body. She also stresses the importance of self-care to a healthy and magical life, with guidance on empowering steps you can take to bring yourself into better energetic balance.

The greater part of the book provides a comprehensive introduction to each of the seven chakras, from root to crown. You'll learn to identify signs of balance and imbalance in each chakra, and discover what you can do to clear energetic blocks and restore balance, both within each chakra and throughout the body as a whole. You'll also learn about how energy healing, specifically in the form of Reiki, can create real, positive changes in your body, mind, and spirit. (Please note, however, that none of the information in this book is intended as medical advice.)

this understanding of the body, each in their own way, but unless we're raised with this knowledge, we have to seek it out on our own.

Luckily, more and more people *have* been discovering the magic of the body, and applying what they've learned for the benefit of themselves and others. We have more access to information and to truly holistic healing modalities than ever before. One major influence on this paradigm shift is the ancient Hindu concept of the chakras, or energy centers, that move energy throughout the body. These seven key points of energy help the body and mind function at their optimal level. When properly understood, they can be seen as a road map to overall well-being of your mind, body, and spirit.

In recent decades, the chakras have gained much-deserved attention among Western alternative healers. Practitioners of modalities like Reiki, therapeutic touch, craniosacral therapy, and many other methods have integrated the concept of the chakras into their approach to healing. The healer I work with draws from her knowledge of the chakras and the meridians (another component of the body's energy system) as well as her experience as a chiropractor to free up blocked energy and promote healing at the physical, emotional and spiritual levels. I am now accustomed to feeling that magic she initially described, and experiencing life on a deeper level than ever.

Not surprisingly, witches of all stripes have also incorporated the chakras into their practice in one way or another. For example, they may use crystals that correspond in color with one or more chakras in healing spells, or visualize activating their chakras in meditation.

PREFACE

A little while ago, at my first appointment, my energy healer asked me what I do for a living. "Okay," she said, after I told her. "So you know a lot about magic. How about on a physical level—do you experience magic inside your body?"

I had to think about that for a minute. In the context of ritual and spellwork, I'm definitely connecting and interacting with a perceivable energy. And in my daily life, I am very often connected on a psychic level with my guides and ancestors. But she was asking a different question: to what extent was I experiencing spiritual energy on the inside, as something originating *within* me, rather than something seemingly external that I'm connecting to? Did I feel that kind of magic?

I had to conclude that I hadn't. Yet.

It turns out that most humans alive today, especially in Western societies, haven't felt that kind of magic either. Most of us, including experienced witches, are not aware of how ingenious, resilient, and regenerative the physical body is designed to be, and *can* be when supported in ways that facilitate its own inherent magic. There have been cultures and spiritual traditions throughout the world that do hold

Ajna Out of Balance..*115*
Methods of Opening and Balancing Your
Third Eye Chakra..*118*
Herbs for the Third Eye Chakra.................................*121*

Chapter Nine: Crown Chakra, Sahasrara **122**

Sahasrata Out of Balance..*125*
Herbs for the Crown Chakra......................................*128*
Exercise for the Crown Chakra...................................*128*

Chapter Ten: Reiki for Balancing and Healing **130**

Distance Reiki 134

Conclusion **138**

Suggestions for Further Reading................................*139*
About the Authors...*140*

Herbs for the Root Chakra... 70
A Root Chakra Exercise.. 71
A Root Chakra Tea.. 73

Chapter Four: Sacral Chakra, Swadhisthana..................... 75

Swadhisthana and Western Culture............................ 76
Journal Therapy.. 79
Exercise and the Sacral Chakra................................... 80
Herbs for the Sacral Chakra... 81
A Simple Sacral Chakra Recipe................................... 82

Chapter Five: Solar Plexus Chakra, Manipura 84

Manipura Out of Balance... 86
Herbs for the Solar Plexus Chakra............................... 87
Exercise and the Solar Plexus Chakra......................... 88
Solar Plexus Chakra Herbal Bath................................. 89

Chapter Six: Heart Chakra, Anahata................................... 93

Anahata Out of Balance... 96
Journal Therapy.. 99
Herbs for the Heart Chakra.. 99
Tea and Ceremony for the Heart Chakra 100

Chapter Seven: Throat Chakra, Vishuddha 103

Vishuddha Out of Balance.. 105
Journal Therapy... 108
Herbs for the Throat Chakras 108
Clearing Your Throat Tea... 109
Vocal Exercises for Clearing and
Claiming Your Voice 110

Chapter Eight: Third Eye Chakra, Ajna 111

CONTENTS

Preface 10

Prologue: Magic and the Body 14

   Spellwork and Shadows 16
   Trauma and Energy 18
   Magic and the Chakras 21

Introduction 26

Chapter One: Energy and the Seven Chakras 31

   The Seven Chakras 33
   The Chakras and Holistic Medicine 40
   The Chakras and Kundalini 43

Chapter Two: Healing, Supporting, and
Balancing the Chakras 45

   Self-Care is Essential to Well-Being 46
   Feeding and Moving Your Body 48
   Rest and Mindfulness 51
   Keeping a Balanced Mindset 54
   General Strategies for Balancing the Seven Chakras 57
   Herbs and the Chakras 60

Chapter Three: Root Chakra, Muladhara 63

   Muladhara Out of Balance 65
   Journal Therapy 67

GET THREE FREE AUDIOBOOKS FROM LISA CHAMBERLAIN

Did you know that all of Lisa's books are available in audiobook format? Best of all, you can get **three audiobooks completely free** as part of a 30-day trial with Audible.

Wicca Starter Kit contains three of Lisa's most popular books for beginning Wiccans, all in one convenient place. It's the best and easiest way to learn more about Wicca while also taking audiobooks for a spin! Simply visit:

www.wiccaliving.com/free-wiccan-audiobooks

Alternatively, *Spellbook Starter Kit* is the ideal option for building your magical repertoire using candle and color magic, crystals and mineral stones, and magical herbs. Three spellbooks —over 150 spells—are available in one free volume, here:

www.wiccaliving.com/free-spell-audiobooks

Audible members receive free audiobooks every month, as well as exclusive discounts. It's a great way to experiment and see if audiobook learning works for you.

If you're not satisfied, you can cancel anytime within the trial period. You won't be charged, and you can still keep your books!

YOUR FREE GIFT

Thank you for adding this book to your Wiccan library! To learn more, why not join Lisa's Wiccan community and get an exclusive, free spell book?

The book is a great starting point for anyone looking to try their hand at practicing magic. The ten beginner-friendly spells can help you to create a positive atmosphere within your home, protect yourself from negativity, and attract love, health, and prosperity.

Little Book of Spells is now available to read on your laptop, phone, tablet, Kindle or Nook device!

To download, simply visit the following link:

www.wiccaliving.com/bonus

Disclaimer

No part of this publication may be reproduced or transmitted in any form or by any means, mechanical or electronic, including photocopying or recording, or by any information storage and retrieval system, or transmitted by email without permission in writing from the publisher.

While all attempts have been made to verify the information provided in this publication, neither the author nor the publisher assumes any responsibility for errors, omissions, or contrary interpretations of the subject matter herein.

This book is for entertainment purposes only. The views expressed are those of the author alone, and should not be taken as expert instruction or commands. The reader is responsible for his or her own actions.

Adherence to all applicable laws and regulations, including international, federal, state, and local governing professional licensing, business practices, advertising, and all other aspects of doing business in the US, Canada, or any other jurisdiction is the sole responsibility of the purchaser or reader.

Neither the author nor the publisher assumes any responsibility or liability whatsoever on the behalf of the purchaser or reader of these materials.

Any perceived slight of any individual or organization is purely unintentional.

Chakras for Witches

Copyright © 2023 by Lisa Chamberlain.

All rights reserved. No part of this book may be reproduced in any form without permission in writing from the author. Reviewers may quote brief passages in reviews

Published by **Chamberlain Publications (Wicca Shorts)**

ISBN-13: 978-1-912715-87-9

believe on some level that money is bad and wanting it is somehow wrong. This is common for those who grew up in families where money was a chronic source of tension or arguments, and for people who believe they can't be "spiritual" and wealthy at the same time.

When it comes to healing spells, obstacles to success can be both obvious and subtle. It's definitely challenging to visualize feeling great when you feel lousy, for example, or when dealing with a recurring issue that's been frustrating you for a long period of time. But it's important to recognize that illnesses or imbalances can be the body's way of alerting us to something deeper that's longing to be acknowledged and healed. And that "something" is likely affecting other areas of our lives as well, such as our relationships or our sense of material security.

When we have unresolved trauma, repressed emotions, or other unconscious blocks in our energy field, or aura, simply knowing how to do spellwork isn't enough to solve the problem. We need to clean up our energy so we can get in alignment with our goals. This could involve working with a mental health counselor, an energy healer, a spiritual advisor, a life coach, or another holistically-minded professional, but it can also just be a matter of self-exploration, meditation, and journaling.

Regardless of the specific tools and methods used, people who earnestly engage in a healing journey often find that as they clear their unconscious blocks and release old energies, the problems they've been dealing with in other areas of life also resolve, without any magical workings required. Indeed, working for healing, whether it's physical, mental, or emotional, can be very fertile ground for self-discovery and major life upgrades.

TRAUMA AND ENERGY

The word "trauma" often brings to mind life-threatening and/or tragic events. People who haven't had such experiences may believe that they've never experienced trauma, but in reality, there are countless stressful situations that can cause traumatic responses in a person. Some people experience vastly more trauma than others, but no one who makes it into an Earthly incarnation escapes trauma altogether.

In fact, being born is the first trauma we experience. Even if we aren't physically injured in the process, we're still rather suddenly thrust from the warm, dark safety of the womb into a completely unfamiliar world. Some psychologists believe that babies who cry incessantly or are often sick are responding to painful memories of their birth experience. Others theorize that this initial trauma, if not resolved through proper care in the first weeks and months after birth, can set the stage for all kinds of anxieties and issues throughout our lives.

Traumatic events can be acute and physical, such as a bad fall, a car accident, or a violent assault. But many people, especially sensitive types, also experience what could be called "subtle" trauma. This can include growing up in a physically safe but emotionally dysfunctional home, being chronically ridiculed or picked on at school, or simply feeling "different" and therefore misunderstood by most of the people in your life.

Subtle trauma can also be experienced vicariously, through witnessing other people in distressing situations. We may witness such things personally, but we can also put ourselves in a traumatized state simply by paying too much attention to the news!

It's important to recognize that trauma is not actually the event or situation in question, but the wound to the psyche that results. For this reason, trauma is relative, and everyone experiences it in their own way. What may be traumatic for one person might be merely unpleasant for another.

But we've all had experiences that caused feelings we didn't want to feel. It's natural to try to shut down negative emotions rather than feel them, let them run their course, and then let them go. But when we repress or try to escape unpleasant emotions, we only relegate them to the shadow side of ourselves, where they can run amok with our physical, mental, emotional, and even spiritual health.

All of us have some degree of "shadow stuff" lurking within. It just goes with the territory of being human. The question is whether or not we want to keep carrying it around. And by "carrying it around," I'm not just speaking metaphorically. It turns out that we carry the energies of these unwanted experiences, emotions, beliefs, and memories not just in our subconscious minds, but also in our physical bodies. This is the "mind-body-spirit" connection that so many holistic healers talk about.

We are not merely physical beings, but spiritual beings inhabiting physical bodies, experiencing life through thoughts and emotions. These nonphysical factors of our experience—the mental, emotional, and spiritual levels of existence—are still experienced while in a physical body, and are therefore relevant to our physical health as well. When too much repressed emotional energy is present, the physical body will eventually manifest imbalances, or illness. We may not even know these energy blocks are there, until we get a serious diagnosis.

MAGIC AND THE CHAKRAS

Working with the chakras is a subtle but powerful way to dislodge our unconscious blocks and get our energy moving in a healthy flow through our bodies. The chakra system can be thought of as a map of our whole self that we can use to locate and identify our imbalances, and begin working to address them. Depending on our situation, we don't even necessarily have to consciously remember the events that caused the blocks—we simply need to listen to our bodies, allow whatever feelings are coming up to be felt and released, and make any changes our bodies are asking for.

Intentionally working to resolve our energetic blocks can bring us to a balanced, stable, clear-minded place from which to work our best magic. As Leandra puts it:

"Magick is the act of focused will. Some compare it to prayer, yet I see it as being something far more interactive than merely asking a higher power to take over and cure all your ills. Magick is what we use to manifest what we desire through action, both metaphysical and physical. If you cannot make a direct and balanced connection between all the aspects—mind, body, emotion, and spirit—

your magick will almost always fall short or fail altogether. This is not to say that chakras are the key, but they are a great focal point to start establishing focus and balance within your practice."

I have a friend who prefers to work magic when he's angry, rather than from a calm and centered place. He says the anger helps him connect with his personal power. He understands the principle of "do no harm," and would never work to directly harm anyone, but he will use manipulative magic at times. He's a powerful witch who gets results, but they come with fairly serious blowback.

For example, he once had an argument with a new neighbor who was building a high fence next door. When finished, the fence was going to block out a view he'd enjoyed ever since he'd moved in, over a decade ago. After the confrontation with the neighbor, my friend worked a spell called "Return to Sender." A few days later, he received a letter from his landlords informing him that they were selling the house he lived in, and he had to move out as soon as possible. Well, that was one way to avoid the problem of the fence, but it wasn't what he had in mind!

To buy himself some time as he searched for new housing, my friend worked another spell to "freeze" the situation. This time, he made spell poppets representing his landlords and put them in his freezer. He did end up with an extension on his move-out date, but not before getting into a costly car accident, right in front of the house!

I've discussed with him, of course, the energetic relationship between what he sends out and what he gets back in return. He understands it logically, but doesn't see a way around it, because he believes he can't fully access his own power without the anger. My friend had a lot of family dysfunction going on when he was a teenager. As a result, he has a lot of emotional pain stuck in his body. Try as he might, he hasn't been able to access a higher-frequency energy state that would allow him to work more harmonious and effective magic.

In terms of the energy of the body, I would guess that my friend is working from his solar plexus chakra, which is associated with willpower, choices, control, and the element of fire. But his heart chakra has been blocked for many years, leaving him unable to fully access his empathy and compassion for others, especially people he perceives himself to be in conflict with.

A blocked heart chakra, as you will learn in Chapter 6, also compromises the balance of the upper chakras—the throat, third eye, and crown. This "domino effect" further prevents my friend from accessing the higher states of consciousness that would allow him to see a better magical path to the solutions he's seeking. Balancing his energy flow through the chakras would help him release the stuck emotional energy from his field and empower him to make better decisions.

The most successful magic always comes from a balanced, *embodied* state of awareness. This doesn't mean you can't have any success in spellwork if you're out of balance, but that the more balanced your energy is, the fewer limitations there will be on your ability to align with the energetic frequency of your magical goal. In other words, when you're living more fully in alignment with your higher self, you've got much more power for manifesting your dreams.

Of course, the point of healing and balancing your chakras isn't just to be more proficient at magic, but to live a happier, healthier life (which is arguably the underlying goal of magic in the first place). When we're working with the energy of the body, we can experience physical, mental, and emotional healing that lead to benefits in all areas of our lives, including at the spiritual level. Given that spiritual growth is also part of the path of witchcraft, it's no wonder that more and more witches have embraced the concept of the chakras and integrated this kind of work into their practice.

As a witch and an energy healer, Leandra is an ideal guide for our journey of discovery into the energy of the body, the role the chakras play in our overall well-being, and the possibilities for healing they have to offer us if we will listen to their messages.

As you read the descriptions of the chakras and their significance to the way you have been experiencing life, you will likely have moments of recognition with some (or a lot) of what you encounter here. This can be a powerfully enlightening experience, but it may also feel disheartening at first. You may feel some judgment toward yourself, or even a sense of shame about having these issues, or not being able to see them for what they were until now.

Alternatively, if you've experienced a lot of trauma and you're aware of it, you may experience anger and desire to blame other people (like your parents, your teachers, an ex-partner, or that one nasty bully in your middle school) for the place you find yourself in now. Or you may just feel a sense of injustice, a sense that life has not been fair to you. These are all normal reactions to learning more about yourself, your body, and the challenges we face as humans trying to live healthy, peaceful, and authentic lives.

The truth is, there's no need for blame or shame or even regret when it comes to how you got to where you are now, because everything you've experienced has led you to this moment, where positive change can happen. You are exactly where you're supposed to be at this point on your own journey—right here, reading a book you sense can provide you with the tools you need for your next steps.

Be kind to yourself. Know that you are worthy of healing and living a more fulfilled and magical life. You deserve it.

Blessed Be.

INTRODUCTION

When I first was introduced to the idea of working with chakras, the whole thing felt weird and "hinky" to me. In retrospect, this was to be expected. I am a Westerner, and like many Americans, I was taught by our culture to be skeptical of things that seem obscure. Even though I was born and raised in Southern California, where "non-traditional" ideas seem to be more readily accepted, I found that embracing something outside my "norm" was difficult.

Additionally, I had moved to South Central Pennsylvania, where new ideas, open-mindedness, and innovations are not common. In fact, most alternative ideas and healing modalities are thought of as woo-woo here, and often they are fiercely refused.

I was working as an Executive Administrative Assistant for a decidedly professional company, and this was definitely not a place where seeking things outside the box was accepted. The office gave me the nickname "Trail Mix" because I was not afraid to try the sushi restaurant down the road or bring a mango or avocado to work with lunch. Being closed-minded is not me. As a result, I was insulted and belittled whenever my co-workers found the opportunity.

At the time, I had been actively practicing Wicca for a few years, and I was learning more about Eastern philosophy and healing modalities. Of course, if anyone nearby overheard conversations with my closest friends, it was enough to set them on edge.

The idea that you can heal and balance a person (or yourself) using energy from your hands, and through focusing on specific energy centers within the body, was entirely against the social environment I found myself swimming (or, rather, drowning) in. This environment reinforced my natural skepticism, and I felt like I needed to question everything I studied.

My name is Leandra Witchwood, and I am a practicing Witch with over 25 years of working experience. I am also a Master Herbalist, Usui Reiki Master, and a Celtic Reiki Master. I currently hold 2 diplomas as a Master Herbalist, and I'm a shadow work coach.

How did I go from "That's weird! No thanks!" to earning two Reiki Masteries and making energy healing a part of my life and business? Well, it wasn't easy, that's for sure! Naturally, at first, I was on the defensive. Only after I allowed myself to let my guard down was I able to discover the knowledge within my reach.

When I began to dig deep and open myself to learn, I quickly realized that there is a universe of knowledge out there, and I was interested! Yep, the same knowledge I assumed was "hinky" stuff was not so hinky after all. For one thing, these philosophies have been around for many thousands of years! Time tested modalities say a lot when you get down to it. It doesn't matter if your social conditioning refuses them; the culture they were derived from ensures their validity.

Maybe it is the Pisces in me, but I have always wanted to know more than what I was spoon-fed by others. For as long as I can remember, I have needed to understand esoteric concepts on an intimate level. This drove my Christian counselors and ministers crazy! In my experience, if you asked about the deeper "why" behind the church's teachings and motivations, you were somehow challenging the church itself. To the fear-filled, this was blasphemy.

Of course, sometimes the message of "Stop asking questions!" would stick, and I would quietly crawl into my cave to pout. Even then, I still could not stand only knowing the basics of what I was taught or expected to comprehend. It all felt too shallow and meaningless when I was refused more profound knowledge. So I continued to ask more questions.

I found every contradiction and asked for an explanation. I found every hypocrisy and asked for the reason. I was often punished for my audacity. My behavior (or, rather, curiosity) was viewed as "disrespectful." Eventually, I was shunned by the church. You know what? I am so glad they chose to turn their backs on me. Their inability to teach me, and allow me to be curious, eventually drove me to find my true path.

The point here is that blind faith is not my thing. Over the years, I have found that questioning and probing only further solidifies my convictions. What I once thought was hinky and off-limits is now part of my truth. I would never have reached this level of positive balance and peace in my life if I had simply complied. Questioning has allowed me to know my faith and my path, inside and out.

Perhaps you are here because you, too, want to know more. Maybe you have been working on healing and balancing your life, but you feel like there is still something missing—a puzzle piece that will help everything come together. I hear you! You crave in-depth knowledge, and that is why we have come together!

In this book, we will focus on the whole, or the holistic view of healing. After all, holistic wellness and health are about caring for the mind, body, and spirit together. We do not see them as being separate. They are all considered and cared for together because they are all connected. To reach a state of balance, each must be addressed with wholeness as intended within the holistic model.

Within these pages, I want to help you gain an understanding of some of the basics when it comes to knowing and working with the chakras. I will walk you through some of my practices and understandings about chakras, herbs, energy work, and more.

I like to take a unique approach to working with chakras. In addition to using Reiki energy healing, I use herbs and blend them into teas. Then I use a ceremony or ritual which combines my knowledge into a unique mix that often looks very different compared to most traditional practitioners. I also take these techniques to women's retreats and gatherings where I share my practices with others.

I hope you enjoy my take on working with the chakras, and how to work toward balancing and healing each one. I want to give you the ability to take the knowledge I offer and use it to fuel your spiritual and healing needs. I also hope this inspires you to strike out and find your own unique blend of magick and philosophy. Creating balance in our lives and within our energy is not a destination. Instead, it is a process—a journey that brings you to a greater understanding because the journey has so much to offer.

Chapter One:
ENERGY AND THE SEVEN CHAKRAS

Energy is a fun thing. It tends to follow the path of least resistance and can sometimes be unpredictable. The energy flowing through your chakras is like water coming through your household pipes. Eventually, the water you request will flow out of the desired tap where it can be used.

The water we get from our pipes is clean, dependable, and on-demand for our everyday needs: hydrating our bodies, brushing our teeth, taking showers, washing clothes, and even flushing the toilet. Walk over to the nearest faucet and turn it on. Right now, you are literally controlling the flow of energy that presents itself in the form of water. Okay, now turn that off! We don't like wasting water here.

Talented plumbers and engineers figured out a long time ago how to provide every home with clean, dependable water on demand, straight from the faucet. Just turn on the tap and there you go! The only time this clean water becomes restricted is when you don't pay your water bill, or when the systems that keep it clean and flowing are in disrepair and neglect. If you have ever experienced a natural disaster where access to clean water was limited or unavailable, you can understand the value water has in our lives.

I was born and raised in Southern California, and I have had my share of earthquakes. I remember one quake in 1987 that shocked the whole state. At the time, I lived about 20 miles from the epicenter. Even at that distance, the earthquake hit our little town hard. The violent shaking of this quake managed to shift some water pipes in our town just enough to allow mud and dirt to mix with our clean water.

Many homes, mine included, were without clean running water for a few days. We had to buy bottled water to perform our everyday activities, like brush our teeth and bathe. In this situation, I consider my family lucky compared to people in other parts of the world, where water has been disrupted for weeks and months due to natural disasters. When you go without a vital resource for a while, you quickly learn its importance in your everyday life, and how easily it can be taken for granted.

Over time, I have also discovered that if you never knew how good things could be or how easy things could be for you in life, you don't know what you are missing. If you have lived most of your life with blocked or sluggish chakras, you have no idea how great you can feel with unblocked and balanced chakras. You won't know how good you can feel until you do the work to free up your energy.

THE SEVEN CHAKRAS

The theology and practice of working with chakras originated in Eastern spirituality and yogi traditions. The chakras were first mentioned in the Vedas, the oldest collection of Hindu scriptures and hymns dating back to approximately 1500–1700 BCE. These four texts form the basis of ancient yogi traditions. Through the ancient theologies and practices found in the Vedic texts, we have developed our modern Western understanding of yogic practices, the chakras, and Kundalini energy (more on this below).

As you might already know, there are seven major chakras, or energy centers, in the body. These centers radiate their energy through and around your body, including the immediate area outside of your physical body, which is often called the "subtle body," the "energy body" or the "luminous body." The subtle body is really a series of layers of energy which all interact with the physical body and with each other. Together, these subtle energy bodies are known as the aura.

It is believed that the energy of each chakra flows out into our aura, and each chakra can influence our mood, our ability to heal (physically, mentally & emotionally), our ability to express love, and even our ability to connect with Divinity.

The chakras are believed to run up the spine, starting at the tailbone all the way up the top of the head and just above your head. Each chakra has a specific association, or governing place, within the body. The chakras also correspond with specific organs, glands within the endocrine system, and other vital systems within the body. Each chakra is associated with a color, the order of which follows the color spectrum of the rainbow, beginning with the root chakra.

The Root Chakra

Sanskrit name: Muladhara
Governing location: base of spine/tailbone, first three vertebrae
Color: red
Element: Earth
Psychological and behavioral functions:
- Basic survival (food, sleep, shelter, self-preservation, etc.)
- Sense of safety and security
- Physicality concerning how you show up in the world
- Physical identity and aspects of self
- Ability to ground

The Sacral Chakra

Sanskrit name: Swadhisthana
Governing location: lower abdomen, reproductive organs
Color: orange
Element: Water
Psychological and behavioral functions:
- Sexuality

- Emotions, feelings
- Relationships and relating to others
- Sensual pleasure
- Creativity
- Fantasies

The Solar Plexus Chakra

Sanskrit name: Manipura
Governing location: navel to the upper torso
Color: yellow
Element: Fire
Psychological and behavioral functions:
- Self-confidence
- Self-motivation
- Courage
- Willpower & self-control
- The ability to speak up for yourself
- Sense of purpose
- Reliability
- Sense of responsibility

The Heart Chakra

Sanskrit name: Anahata
Governing location: heart, shoulders, arms
Color: green
Element: Air
Psychological and behavioral functions:
- Unconditional love
- Self-love
- Self-care
- Compassion/empathy
- Connectedness

The Throat Chakra

Sanskrit name: Vishuddha
Governing location: throat, neck, head (up to the eyes)
Color: blue
Element: Akasha/Ether
Psychological and behavioral functions:
- Self-expression
- Speaking your truth
- Speaking clearly
- Able to convey your needs to others
- Integrity
- Innovation
- Authenticity

The Third Eye Chakra

Sanskrit name: Ajna
Governing location: middle of the eyebrows, forehead, and head
Color: purple or indigo
Element: Light
Psychological and behavioral functions:
- Intuition
- Perception
- Wisdom
- Inspiration
- Creativity
- Psychic ability/awareness

The Crown Chakra

Sanskrit name: Sahasrara
Governing location: top of head, and just above the head
Color: white or violet and gold

Element: Intelligence
Psychological and behavioral functions:
- Divine connection
- Sense of unity
- Trust in the Divine
- Sense of being part of something bigger

Like a faucet that has been turned on, when you unblock and heal your chakras, you turn on your essence, or inner power. You open your floodgates to your higher self and your ability to tap into your authenticity. When you take care of yourself and ensure your energy centers are well maintained, you will have all the energy you need for healing, creativity, prosperity, and establishing positive change in your life.

A lack of flow is what happens when an energy center, or chakra, becomes imbalanced. An imbalance can occur when we experience trauma or neglect, physically, emotionally, and psychologically. Often, events and experiences from our childhood are the culprits of either restricted or hyper energy flow from our chakras. Sometimes we are unable to deal with our past trauma and issues positively. In this case, we tend to adopt negative or unproductive coping mechanisms, which can create an even more significant imbalance, making our energy flow erratic or nearly nonexistent.

When we have blockages, think of it like sludge in your pipes or a clogged toilet. (I know, "*gross!*") In this case, you can try to turn on the faucet or flush the toilet all you want, but nothing is going to happen. If you have an overly active energy center, think of it as a leak in the pipe, with energy spewing everywhere. Whether it's a block or a leak, this energy imbalance will continue so long as you continue to ignore or dismiss the issue that is causing it.

When the chakras are imbalanced, we will often experience a multitude of issues or symptoms. Some of these issues we experience have been with us most of our life, making them very difficult to pinpoint and address. Over time, these imbalances simply became part of our routine, or mode of operation.

When a behavior, pain, or way of being has been with you for as long as you can remember, it is easy to view it as part of who you are. When something has become part of who you think you are, you may find it very hard to let go of this issue, mindset, or behavior. After all, because you have lived with it for so long, you may not know how to live or exist without it, whatever "it" may be.

Maybe you have trouble waking up in the morning, and you have decided that because this has always been your mode of operation, that you are just not a morning person. Or perhaps you have a lack of motivation when it comes to achieving your dreams, and because you have lived with this mindset for so long, you have simply accepted that you are not an easily motivated person. Maybe you experience low back pain, or heartburn, and so on, which can all become part of your way of being, without you knowing there could be another way. These mindsets and issues go back as far as you can remember, so how can you imagine another way of living?

If you are able to zoom out and see things from a different perspective, you will learn that your symptoms and counterproductive mindsets are trying to tell you something. Often, they are trying to tell you that something is not right.

They are trying to alert you to something you can alleviate if you choose to do the work. Eventually, if we ignore our symptoms long enough, the imbalance in our energy centers and bodies will move from "dis-ease" to disease.

The heartburn you experience might be telling you that you need to address a simple issue with your esophagus, but if you ignore it for too long, the inflammation can lead to cancer. Or the sensitivity in your tooth might be telling you to see the dentist before you have to get a root canal. Similarly, sluggish metabolism and the inability to speak your mind might be telling you to address the energy imbalance in your throat chakra. The good news is that when you begin to acknowledge the issue, you can then start to treat the problem.

THE CHAKRAS AND HOLISTIC MEDICINE

The idea behind holistic health and well-being is that we treat the whole self, not just the symptoms, and not just the body. With this mindset firmly in our grasp, we take care of the mind, body, and spirit. Many times, ill health and imbalances can be treated with simple methods, like changing your diet. Eating more fruits and vegetables and cutting out fried foods, sugar, and processed foods is #1 on my list of places to begin. (These and many other holistic approaches are discussed in detail in Chapter 2.)

In Western medicine, by contrast, the typical method of treatment has become symptom-based. Instead of digging deep to get to the source of the imbalance, our Western medical mindset is to address what is wrong on the surface. Much of this is because they are pressured and rushed by insurance companies and investors. Their allocation of time and attention for each patient is often dictated by investors and insurance companies, which limit the time each doctor is allowed to spend with patients to create a better bottom line.

As a result, this limited attention creates unnecessary stress on the healthcare provider along with the patient.

Like us, even doctors and nurses need to rest and heal! No one can run from one 15-minute appointment to the next, 50 times a day without taking time to breathe, relax, and recharge. Stress can make us forgetful, and lead us to cut corners, which often ends up costing us more in the long run. In the case of the doctor-patient relationship, patients lose their trust in and respect for their practitioners. Most importantly, they miss out on true healing.

Western medicine has its strengths, particularly when it comes to bodily injuries and acute emergencies. But when it comes to chronic health issues, while you may find some relief and healing from using Western medicine, chances are you will continue to have an underlying feeling like something is still "off." Dealing with the imbalances within your chakra system could very well be the missing puzzle piece.

There are various ways you can work with the chakras. Some keep with the traditional use of yoga, from Kundalini yoga to Vinyasa and Hatha yoga. Some work with meditation to connect with Shakti and Kundalini energy. Some draw, paint, sing, dance, and some use Reiki, a form of energy healing which we will look at in detail in Chapter 10. I use herbs and Reiki in my practice. For me, this combination has been a profound and energizing modality.

When I was taught to work with these energy centers, I was taught to see them as spinning wheels (after all, "chakra" means "wheel" in Sanskrit). I have also worked with Reiki practitioners who view each chakra as individual balls of light. Other practitioners see them as colorful flowers, each having a different number of petals, depending on the chakra. As an herbalist, the flower association makes perfect sense to me, but you choose the visual you prefer for each. When I work with others, I prefer that they choose the concepts that make the most sense to them.

While we address each chakra separately, it is good to understand that they all flow into one another. Because the flow of energy through the physical and luminous body is governed by the health and wellness of each chakra, each chakra plays a role in the balance of the whole. When one is imbalanced, another will become overly active to help compensate. I am a firm believer that if you have one severely imbalanced chakra, the rest will also experience a level of imbalance as compensation, and your emotional and physical health can be directly affected.

As you learn about each chakra, you may find that some aspects of one chakra relate to or seem evident in another. Dichotomous lines drawn between each chakra is not realistic. Energy, like water, will pick up and utilize what it encounters, sometimes becoming muddied in the process. Any lines we draw conceptually between the chakras become blurred as we explore the whole.

THE CHAKRAS AND KUNDALINI

When we work with the seven chakras, you might also begin working with the Kundalini, or Kundalini energy. Kundalini is an energy, or consciousness, which is believed to be our life source. This energy is coiled like a serpent at the base of the spine, about where the root chakra is.

"Kundalini" is a Sanskrit term, but versions of this concept can be found in many indigenous cultures, with ancient artworks depicting a rising snake in the body. This rising happens when the Kundalini energy is awakened, which can be brought about through pursuing spiritual practices (like Kundalini yoga) or happen accidentally, due to life circumstances.

Kundalini is often thought to be female with three aspects. When awakened, she will rise up the spine from the root chakra all the way to the crown. When stimulated, she will provide a massive amount of energy to the chakras and the individual.

Some describe this awakening experience as a feeling of lightning shooting up the spine. Some experience her as a woman dressed in white, like a ghost who seems to be present when the time and need are apparent. She will also bring the individual to a new perspective. Many say nothing is ever the same once you experience Kundalini awakening.

To me, Kundalini is a Goddess, one to be respected as we work through our chakras. Her energy cannot be forced or demanded upon. Her three aspects represent the three aspects of the spiritual journey: the lower, mid, and higher self. When in balance, all three aspects can work together to create healing and balance.

No matter how you experience her or receive her, she is energy, and she is infinite in her ability. If you delve into the theology and practice of yoga, awakening Kundalini energy, and chakra healing, you will begin to see their close relationship.

Chapter Two: HEALING, SUPPORTING, AND BALANCING THE CHAKRAS

Before we jump into the practices and techniques I use when working with the chakras, I want to let you know that you're on the right track when it comes to learning about and healing your chakras.

Reading books like this, and adopting the practices you learn as you explore, is a great place to start. When you are looking to make positive changes in your life, every balanced step you take toward health and well-being is the right step. You will make a lot of headway when you dedicate more of your time to your well-being.

SELF-CARE IS ESSENTIAL TO WELL-BEING

I want to be clear that dedicating time to your self-care does not mean you are being selfish. If anything, you are setting yourself up to be more generous than ever before. When you make time to replenish your energy reserves, you have more energy to give to others. You will also find that you can do all of this with less resentment and regret than before. When you take time to heal the holes in your life and lifestyle that leech out your energy, you will find you have more vitality and ability in every aspect of life.

When I first began studying witchcraft, magick, paganism, and other esoteric theologies, I was lucky enough to have a fantastic teacher, who reminded me (over and over) that I cannot pour from an empty cup. She gave us all she could, but she could only do this because she took care of herself. She took time for herself and prioritized her personal healing. There were times of the day when she was unavailable for questions and counseling. This was because she spent this time alone reading, meditating, bathing, etc. This was her self-time. Rarely did she compromise this time.

As I became a mother and eventually a teacher, like my mentor, I too began to realize the importance of taking the time for my own self-care. The excuses I used to make for myself became very evident. Excuses like, "I don't have time to spend alone with myself doing all that self-care crap!" began to sound really ridiculous. Perhaps not so ironically, I hear the same excuse from my students and other members of the community.

We are all swamped. Our culture demands it. We are made to feel inadequate or useless if we are not scheduling every minute of every day. Often, we are expected to provide far more than we have to offer. This forces us to dig deep into our reserves, and as a result, these precious reserves become depleted and completely exhausted. No wonder our chakras are imbalanced and blocked!

In the long run, if we fail to keep our bodies in a healthy condition, we will eventually pay the price. Whether it's gaining excess weight, chronic fatigue, stiff joints, limited flexibility, or poor circulation; we will find that our bodies will break down much easier. When diseases develop, we have reached a point when we have no choice but to take care of ourselves. Our freedom, mobility, range of motion, vitality, and more are gone. If you don't take care of *you* now, your body will force you to do it later.

FEEDING AND MOVING YOUR BODY

You can start with simple changes, like eating a healthier diet. A well-balanced diet is one of the most essential things in every aspect of life. When we treat our bodies well, we have a greater chance of recovery, health, and balance.

Ever wonder how people before the '60s and '70s managed to stay slim compared to our current national average? Think about it—before diets and fitness became a thing, gyms were only used by athletes. The average person didn't take yoga, Pilates, Spinning, or Zumba classes, nor did they spend hours in the gym each week. One big difference between today and decades past is in the amount of food we eat. Our portion sizes are much larger compared to 40 or 50 years ago. Plus, on average, we tend to eat far more processed and fast foods now than ever before.

Sugar is one of the main ingredients in most processed foods, making our diets way off balance. Here is the thing. Sugarcane is actually an incredibly healthy plant to eat, yet the refining process that brings us granulated sugar strips all the health benefits from the plant, making sugars a terrible addition to our diets. The same goes for other refined sugars made from other plants.

Our bodies love to store sugar. Microbes, like bacteria, also *love* sugar. Too much sugar will create a more than welcoming environment for a variety of diseases and dis-ease, which causes issues in the body, like inflammation. Too much inflammation over a long time creates severe health conditions, like chronic fatigue, certain cancers, heart disease, diabetes, sinusitis, rheumatoid arthritis, Alzheimer's, Crohn's disease….and the list goes on.

Sugar is only one example of how the foods we eat affect our well-being. Think of the food you eat as medicine for your body and fuel for your livelihood. Are you eating the food that supports your body's health, or food that will support your body's dis-ease? Vegetables are crucial when trying to establish and maintain balance. Try making most of your meals filled with fresh, unprocessed vegetables, lean protein, and some fruit. Additionally, be sure to drink lots of water and herbal teas as often as you can.

Keep in mind, this does not mean you need to be 100% perfect, 100% of the time. When you work to make positive life-changes try focusing on being consistent 80 to 90% of the time. If you can manage 5 or 6 days of healthy eating per week, you are well on your way to creating a sustainable life change.

Many suggest a vegetarian or vegan lifestyle, and some claim you cannot heal yourself until you adopt this lifestyle. This is absolutely *not* necessary. You need to take care of your body using the foods that are best for your unique physiology. There is no cookie-cutter diet or single method that will get everyone into a healthy state. You must choose what works best for your body and your needs.

In addition to your diet, how often you move will play a role in healing, balancing, and maintaining your healthy chakra flow. Another difference between today and decades past is in the amount of movement people experienced each day. There was a time when the average person spent a lot more time being active. When I was a kid, most of our time was spent outside riding bikes, playing hide and seek, playing kickball, and more. Today we spend far less time moving and far too much time sitting.

Try incorporating ways to get more movement into your life. For example, park farther away from store entrances to get some extra steps in. If you spend the majority of your time sitting at your job, make sure you take a break every hour and stretch. If you can install an under-desk treadmill at your computer, do it. That way, you can walk while you work. You can also try taking a quick 10-minute walk around the building. Maybe you head to the stairs and walk up and down the stairs a few times to get your blood pumping. You can also run if you like—that is entirely up to you!

Take care of your back and muscles. Stretch or practice yoga a few minutes each day. Do some planks and lunges. Go to the park and take a stroll. Go hiking and biking. Dance, jog, hike, take a fitness class, or incorporate another form of exercise. Please don't get me wrong—this does not mean you need to become a gym rat. You don't need to start lifting huge weights and grunting like a giant bear. Instead, simply do activities that get you moving more often, in ways that help you feel good.

REST AND MINDFULNESS

In addition to diet and exercise, resting is an important aspect of maintaining balance and focus. If we don't take time to rest and restore our energy every day, we are robbing ourselves of quality life. Often, this means taking time to slow down, breathe, and relax. It also means taking the time to check in with ourselves to see what we truly need. Do we need a nap? Or perhaps water? Maybe we need to just sit in silence for a while. It's about taking time to allow your body and mind to communicate so they can work better, in better harmony with one another.

We can use our breath to help focus our energy and settle our mind or mental chatter. An example is the "5-5-5" breathing exercise. This is where you breathe in for a count of five, hold this breath for a count of five, and then exhale for a count of five. Try it now: Breathe in one… two… three… four… five… and hold for one… two… three… four… five…. Now release the breath for a count of one… two… three… four… five.

Breathing exercises are simple, yet very useful when it comes to settling our energy, mind, and emotions. Science has shown that when you take time to consciously breathe, you can adjust your brain activity, moving from stress and anxiety into a calmer state of being. Breathing mindfully helps control the autonomic nervous system. The autonomic nervous system regulates individual body systems or processes that work automatically, such as blood pressure, heart rate, body temperature, electrolytes, stress responses, digestion, and more.

In the yogi tradition, breath is used to help the movement of spirit and as a means for raising spiritual awareness. Pranayama (which is a significant element in yoga) is the use of breathing techniques and exercises for various purposes. When we understand the importance of breath in yogi traditions (and other spiritual traditions from around the world), we begin to see the connection breath has to our whole self. In many cultures all over the world, the words for "spirit" and "breathwork" are often interchangeable. *Prana* is a great example. It means "spirit" and "breath," and breath is used to move the energy of spirit.

When we use breathing exercises, we can almost instantly feel how they help reduce stress. Using our breath intentionally in everyday life helps reduce cortisol levels, allowing us to think more clearly and make better decisions. Breathing exercises help us move brain activity from the emotional (or knee-jerk) reactive state to a more relaxed and productive state.

You can try the 5-5-5 exercise any time you feel anxious, stressed, or chaotic. You will notice a significant adjustment in your ability to think and process the situation when you do. The key is remembering to utilize breathing techniques when you need them most. Over time you will begin to use them automatically, creating for yourself a healthy habit.

Another habit you can create for yourself—and one of the most important—is spending time alone. I do this every day. I am usually the first one up in my household. When I get up, I head downstairs and into my meditation/Moon Room. This is a space I claimed for myself. Well, the cats seem to like it too, and I'm cool with that. This room is where I go to be alone, meditate, and practice yoga. It is essential to find or create a space where you can be alone with yourself. Maybe it's a place outside, or even a closet, if that's all you can find. It doesn't matter, as long as you can be undisturbed by others during your alone time.

KEEPING A BALANCED MINDSET

Another good habit to create for yourself is to balance your mindset or attitude. This is not only good for your health, but it helps you navigate difficult situations with less stress. For example, the Moon Room I mentioned above came about as a result of what was initially a disaster: a car crashed into the side of our new house, which destroyed our sunroom.

It happened on a rainy Fourth of July. It was a Saturday, and because of the rain, we canceled our plans to move into our new home. The delay irritated me much. At the time, putting off big projects like this was a massive inconvenience for me. I had things mapped out in my head, and when we had to deviate, I got annoyed. Then worry would set in. I worried the move would somehow fall through. At the time, I thought the best thing I could do for myself was to keep busy. "Don't think about it, and everything will be fine. Don't think about it, so I won't find even more things to worry about that can go wrong."

We were in our old house packing boxes when we got a call from our soon-to-be neighbors (who also happen to be my in-laws). They said there had been an accident and we needed to come to the new house right away. When we arrived, we saw it: a car had crashed into the side of our new house and was currently parked inside our sunroom.

Our driveway was blocked by a fire truck, ambulance, and police cars (in addition to the car *inside* my house!). Soon the rest of the neighborhood was coming outside in the rain to see what happened. We parked our car at my in-law's house and walked down to the accident.

My first thought was, "OMG!" I was already annoyed that we had to hold off on moving and *now this*! I couldn't even comprehend what I was seeing. How does something like this happen? It's not like the house jumped out in front of her! There was a literal car in my house!

Then, as the reality set in, I was glad we decided to hold off on moving that day, for two particular reasons. The first is that my son loved playing in that room. Well before we scheduled our moving day, my husband and I spent our free time working on the new house, and this room was my son's spot to play. He would hang out and play with his toys in the exact place where a car now sat! With this realization, I was glad we postponed and chose to stay at our old house to pack.

The other reason is that if we had gone ahead with the move that day, the moving truck would have been parked in the driveway. It would have been almost in the direct path of this new four-wheeled addition to our home. The driver could have hit our huge moving truck, and likely one of us as we unloaded the truck. She also would have had a higher potential of being killed herself.

As it was, she walked away with no injury, but her car was toast. Her engine block mounts snapped on impact and left my sunroom filled with oil and other fluids. Even after the car was removed, the fluids remained, leaving an unpleasant smell.

During this time, I was in the process of implementing ways to adjust my mindset and how I think of things (especially difficult stuff). In looking for ways to see the benefit of this seemingly horrible situation, I began to see possibility instead of damage and destruction. I began to envision a room I could make my own, to claim this space for myself. This is how my moon room came to be.

It took a long time to come to fruition. We had to work our way through the insurance companies and then through the repairs. This was another opportunity to get my head on straight. Instead of seeing the delays as time-wasters, I saw them as opportunities to save money so I could decorate this room to my liking. It gave me time to slowly buy the curtains, furniture, carpet, etc. that would eventually make this Moon Room magickal.

Once the room was repaired, I made this space entirely serene. I decorated it with long curtains covering the large windows. I draped fabric on the ceiling, swaged low to make the room feel cozy and quiet. Ultimately, what was once a stinking disaster transformed, through a balanced mindset, into something beautiful and fulfilling.

GENERAL STRATEGIES FOR BALANCING THE SEVEN CHAKRAS

In addition to diet, exercise, and mindfulness practices, there are several other strategies you can integrate into your life that will help you maintain the balance you're working to establish. Here is a brief list of activities you can consider as part of your regular routine:

- **Fasting:** Intermittent fasting is a great way to rebalance yourself as a whole. Fasting has been used in spiritual practices all over the world as a means of cleansing the body in preparation for connecting with Divinity. When fasting regularly, it is recommended not to fast beyond 16 hours for women and 18 hours for men.

- **Yoga:** This might be obvious since the concept of chakras comes from the yogi tradition. Establishing a daily yoga practice will help your body build strength, flexibility, and more.

- **Color Therapy:** Try visualizing the color the relates to each chakra when you work with them. Some use spinning colored wheels or flowers in their mediations for the same purpose.

- **Crystals and gemstones:** Many crystals and stones have energies that correspond with each chakra. Using something you can see or hold in your hand can create a sense of tangibility that may help you, especially in the beginning.

- **Reiki:** Receive regular Reiki treatments from a certified practitioner. Whether you do this weekly or monthly doesn't matter, as long as it's consistent. Reiki is not mandatory for healing the chakras, but it serves as a great benefit if you choose to utilize this resource. See Chapter 10 for an in-depth discussion of this healing modality.

- **Daily mantras and visualizations:** Repeating mantras and/or affirmations, and visualizing your goal each day, have been proven effective in many studies. Some of the most successful people in the world utilize these practices with amazing results. An example of a mantra or affirmation is, "I know I am guided by my Divine power." Or "I know I am loved, and I offer love in return." You will find example mantra phrases for each chakra in the following chapters, with further discussion in Chapter 9.

- Finally, work to remove the habits and influences in your life that cause you unnecessary stress or make you feel unproductive, lethargic, or down.

Once you establish healing and a positive flow within each chakra, you will gain a renewed sense of balance and peace in your everyday activities.

HERBS AND THE CHAKRAS

People and plants go hand in hand. Together, we have a unique relationship. If you think about it, plants offer us a great benefit and gift. If humans did not exist, most plants would do just fine. However, if plants went extinct, we humans would be in serious trouble. The way I experience plants is through seeing them as generous helpers. They choose to provide us all we need. They provide us with nourishment, medicine, building materials, fuel, and so much more. Through the use of plants, we can establish a window of health and balance in every area of life.

Scientifically, humans have found that plants provide relief and remedy for specific ailments. For example, if you have high blood pressure, try a daily regimen of chamomile after meals; chances are, you will have positive results. Or if you are a woman and find that you suffer from hormonal imbalances, you can try taking ashwagandha regularly, and you will likely find improvement in your fluctuations.

With each of these examples, however, you will notice we observe with a limited perspective that only includes the physical body. When we work with healing the mind, body, and spirit, we are looking at a holistic model, which requires a little broader perspective. If we are to use herbs for the benefit of our physical health, it only makes sense to also use herbs for our spiritual, emotional, and mental health.

With the knowledge I have gained through dedicated study, I have been led to understand how herbs can also be used to help us on so many levels, from healing the physical body to healing the energy centers of the body. This is where the true mystery lies with plants. Pants have a spirit and essence that is unique and sentient.

When we look closely at the use of herbs and the chakras, we can see that each chakra correlates to specific body systems. So do many herbs. This is where the connection between herbs and chakras is made. Each chakra governs particular systems and functions within the mind, body, and spirit. Each herb will also have a dominant action that directly benefits the physical body. But herbs go beyond this to also address the needs of our body's energy. As we learn about each chakra, we can begin to learn what herbs to use and why.

My passion and love have always been with herbs. This passion has grown to incorporate using herbs with energy healing. Brewing tea is absolutely my favorite way to support my self —mind, body, and spirit. Since humans were capable of brewing teas using herbs steeped in water, teas became a heavily relied-upon source for nourishment and healing. To this day, tea remains a staple in human cultures all over the globe. Even my cat loves to drink tea. (I don't know, she is weird!)

Through my passion for tea, I have developed ways to connect with herbs and use tea for balance. Tea is simple and effective when used as a tool for introspection. It helps bring our scattered and erratic thoughts into focus. Tea can be accompanied by the use of mantras/affirmations, mudras, meditation, and more. In our increasingly hectic and stress-filled world, tea offers us a moment to slow down and take note of all that is around us and within us.

As I mentioned in the introduction, I utilize a ceremony to help create transformation using herbs, tea, and energy healing. I guide participants through various exercises, discussions, and activities that bring us into a state of mindfulness where transformation can take place. Within this mindful state of focus, we can discover and reveal our needs and intentions. When we use tea to reflect and relax, tea can offer us a flavor-filled and mindful experience which can be utilized anywhere.

Understanding plants on a profoundly spiritual level takes time. It also takes a level of dedication; many are not ready all at one time. I admit I may not be fully prepared either, and I have been working with plants for decades. I am grateful to have enough knowledge to incorporate them into my life and the lives of others, so we all can benefit. As we dig deeper, I will offer suggestions on how to use herbs with each chakra as you work to unblock, heal, and balance each chakra. I will also offer activities or meditations you can use for each.

Chapter Three: ROOT CHAKRA, MULADHARA

The Root Chakra at a glance:

Sanskrit name: Muladhara
Governing location: base of spine/tailbone, first three vertebrae
Color: red
Element: Earth
Psychological and behavioral functions:
- Basic survival (food, sleep, shelter, self-preservation, etc.)
- Sense of safety and security
- Physicality concerning how you show up in the world
- Physical identity and aspects of self
- Ability to ground

Root Chakra Mantra: "I am…"

"I am safe"
"I am secure"
"I am rooted"
"I am balanced"

Muladhara, or root chakra, is our base chakra, physically located at the base of the spine. This is the fundamental chakra where our basic needs are evaluated and regulated.

Muladhara is where our sense of safety and security, as well as our survival instincts, are seated. This chakra governs our fight or flight instinct, as well as many physiological and unconscious needs or behaviors, including our motivations related to sleeping, eating, and drinking. It governs our feelings of being rooted where we are in life and within our relationships, as well as our sensory perceptions, which plays a role in our ability to become intimate with others.

Physiologically, the root chakra is related to the legs, anus, adrenal glands, tailbone, and the first three vertebrae above the tailbone. The root chakra also governs the colon, kidneys, bones, and muscles, and the arterial blood flow through the left atria, moving oxygen and nutrients throughout the body.

Typically, physical and emotional issues associated with an overactive or imbalanced root chakra include knee and hip issues, foot and ankle issues, eating disorders, weight issues, body image issues, anxiety, and other general feelings of insecurity, both physical and emotional.

If you have a balanced root chakra, you will most likely feel "deeply rooted." You will have a solid sense of security within most things you do, which allows you to feel as though you can live a full life. You might also feel energetic and creative when this chakra is healthy and balanced. Through the root chakra, we gain or achieve our sense of belonging to our environment, home life, relationships, etc. This is our sense of belonging.

Think of the root chakra as energy extending from your tailbone down through your legs and into the earth, like the roots of a tall tree fortified by its ability to dig deep and anchor itself into the earth. We use this visual as a tool to root or ground energy that does not serve us. Through the root chakra, we can become more intimate with the element of earth as we seek to create stability and sustainability in our lives.

This extends to our practice as witches as well. When we are deeply rooted in our beliefs, traditions, and understanding of magick, we can create better efficiency and proficiency in all we set to achieve.

A balanced and effectively active root chakra helps us ground excess or erratic energy. This is especially helpful when we experience anxiety or overwhelming emotional energy. You will find this ability extremely useful, whether you need to ground excess spell energy or anxious energy you experience from being in crowded spaces and the like.

MULADHARA OUT OF BALANCE

An imbalanced or overactive root chakra will have the opposite feeling—you might be the *source* of erratic and unstable energy. You may find that you often feel anxious, insecure, distracted, and as a result, frustrated. You might not be able to pinpoint why you feel this way. Some may just explain these experiences as, "this is just how I am," or "this is how I have always been." The real test of this assumption comes when situations or stressors trigger you to feel and then express overwhelm, leaving you unable to cope with the situation.

Social gatherings and interactions with strangers are especially difficult when the root chakra is imbalanced. You may feel insecure and have low self-esteem, leaving you unable to engage with others. You might feel like you never belong, or that you are an outcast. You may even feel this way in the company of those who share similar interests. As a result, you may find yourself dreading any kind of social gathering, especially ones with a lot of people.

This social insecurity may be something you've always experienced, if you've been out of balance most of your life. Maybe you were always considered the "shy" one of the group. You may find yourself never wanting to leave home because it's easier to avoid strangers and social gatherings altogether. However, this is a double-edged sword, because isolation feeds depression and loneliness. It caters to the imbalance established within. Avoidance creates more imbalance and leaves the issue with your root chakra unresolved.

If your root chakra is imbalanced, you may also find it hard to concentrate. Simple tasks, like reading or listening to a lecture, can become complicated even if the topic is interesting to you. This seems to become most evident when you want to enjoy a book or watch a discussion, but you cannot seem to settle down into a rhythm where you can focus on the words or the person speaking.

Maybe you find yourself rushing through the words looking for a point to be made. Perhaps you have had the feeling for a while now that something is not right, but you can't place your finger on precisely what is happening. This feeling may be fleeting, making it even harder to identify the issue, which causes additional feelings of anxiety and stress. With added anxiety and stress, memory issues can result, leaving us feeling restless and unable to focus.

While an imbalanced root chakra can cause us to feel erratic and unsettled, it can also have the opposite effect, where we experience a complete lack of energy. Low energy and feelings of depression inhibit our ability to act on the things we know need our attention. This conflicted state may trigger anxiety, anger, rage, worry, panic, depression, resentment, frustration, or indifference.

Often, symptoms of an imbalanced root chakra surface as poor focus, disorganized habits, pessimism, and negative or dichotomous thinking. Some may be diagnosed with chronic depression or anxiety. Imbalances in brain chemistry play a part in our overall homeostasis—mentally, physically, emotionally, and spiritually. When we begin to address the imbalances within the whole self, in a true holistic fashion, we can then begin to heal the whole self (mind, body, and spirit) as a result.

JOURNAL THERAPY

The following exercise is meant to help you identify whether you have a blocked root chakra. The critical thing to remember when moving through these questions (and all journal therapies offered in this book) is to refrain from judging yourself and the situation.

This is a time for self-care and self-love, not condemnation. You are doing the best you can with what you have. You can't care for yourself when you are judging yourself or chastising yourself, and others. This is not a time or the place for the "woulda, coulda, shoulda's" of life. At this time, you are not the victim or the martyr. Instead, take the opportunity to identify issues and reflect without judgment or embellishment.

Get out your journal and answer the following questions:

- Do you currently feel secure and stable in your life and relationships?

- Do you have feelings of insecurity? Where and when do these feelings arise?

- Do you experience financial difficulties? Where and when is this evident?

- Do you feel abandoned? Where and when do you feel this way?

- Do you feel "not good enough" regularly? Do you hesitate to offer your opinions, observations, or thoughts on a topic because you fear being ridiculed or discounted? When and where do you feel this way?

If you answered yes to most of these questions, chances are you have a blocked root chakra. The good news is that this can be remedied through the use of simple techniques and awareness. When the root chakra is balanced, energy can flow much like blood flowing through your veins or water through pipes. This frees up your chakras from doing extra work trying to maintain your energy within your daily activities.

Clearing and balancing the energy of your root chakra helps you establish and maintain a sense of belonging, and feel secure in your actions and choices. You will begin to feel more comfortable in social situations and better able to handle difficult situations. You will begin to feel like your choices and opinions matter.

A healthy root chakra will lend you the ability to hold an increased sense of self-worth. Working on this area of your energetic body will help you improve concentration and provide you with clarity in many situations. You will also likely gain the ability to set goals, and the skill to prioritize. Your "monkey mind" (or "squirrel brain") will significantly diminish. From this newly established balance, you will find you are invigorated and passionate about your work and life. You will have a new capacity to love and gain a new sense of motivation in all you do.

After earning my Usui Reiki Master Certification, and when I first began treating others, I decided to test my new skills out at a community Reiki share. I joined another practitioner in treating a young woman who came in to see what a Reiki share was all about. She laid down on the table, and we began her treatment. I took the position at her head and worked my way slowly down to her hips. When I reached this area, I was stopped as a wave of intense energy seemed to tug on my hands. It almost felt like a plug was sucking down water from a very full bathtub.

Soon my head was spinning, and I was feeling a little nauseous. Shocked and a little embarrassed by my inability to see this coming, I quickly tried to regain my stability. When I did recover, I was able to feel the energy draining away from this poor woman. She was radiating anxiety. I spent most of the share on this chakra, and still could not adequately balance it. Her issue was chronic and needed more attention than what I could provide in a short session.

When I opened my eyes, I could now see the physical discomfort this poor girl was experiencing. She was so anxious her upper lip was covered in beads of sweat. When she first came in, I knew she was nervous, but most people who are not familiar with the work we do come in with some form of uncertainty. She, however, was over the top. It was only after I experienced the energy of her root chakra that I understood that this level of anxiety was normal for her.

I asked her how she felt, and with a huge sigh of relief, she said, "WOW, so much better!" "I feel so relaxed!" She went on to explain how she was so nervous about coming in that she almost didn't. She explained that she doesn't like strangers, much less coming into close contact with them. She told me that a friend recommended she try this because her friend was concerned for her.

HERBS FOR THE ROOT CHAKRA

When working with Muladhara chakra, I like to use red herbs and other red plants, such as hibiscus, red tea (like pu-erh or rooibos), rose, red peppers, and red chilis. Foods and herbs that are the color red will help you better connect to the essence of this chakra. The energy of the plants and the vibrational frequency of the color red helps create the energetic connection you need for healing the chakras.

Beyond red herbs and foods, you might also consider other herbs that help balance your body, help relieve anxiety, and improve circulation. Try working with ashwagandha, chamomile, cinnamon, dandelion, garlic, kava-kava, and yarrow.

A ROOT CHAKRA EXERCISE

To help connect with and unblock your Muladhara chakra, you will want to establish safety and security in your surroundings. This is also a great exercise when you want to start the day with confidence and stability.

Ideally, find a place where you know you can conduct this exercise without being disturbed, and without insecurities or fear of judgment. (If you do not have a place to do this at home, because you fear being interrupted or judged, try finding a time when no one is home or when everyone is asleep.) I lay on my floor and perform this exercise before my family wakes up in the morning. In my home, this is the only time I have to myself, making it the perfect opportunity for in-depth work that requires my attention.

You can also do this outside if that works better for you— in fact, I recommend it for added benefit. The point is to find or create a space where you feel safe. You will want to be on the floor or the ground for this exercise. The intention is to root yourself, and being close to the ground helps achieve this.

You will need:

- A yoga or exercise mat. If you don't have either, use a couple of blankets layered on top of each other.
- A pillow or yoga bolster for your legs

- A rolled-up blanket or towel for your head. Avoid using a comforter or other blanket that is too soft. You want something that feels solid and supportive.
- Some soft instrumental music to play (optional)
- Soft lighting, or candles as desired
- Incense, if you desire

Instructions:

Light the candle(s) and incense, if using. Lay your mat or blankets out on the floor. Lie down and arrange your pillow and bolster under your knees. Next, arrange your rolled-up blanket or towel under your head in a way that feels supportive. This is also an excellent time to start playing your music, if you wish.

Now, get comfortable. Make sure your hips and back are anchored and comfortable on the floor. Make sure your head and neck are supported and comfortable as well. Again, the key is to focus on feeling supported and secure in this space you created.

Begin with your breath. As you breathe, feel the floor beneath you. Feel how it supports you and holds you. Also, take a moment to feel how the pillows hold you and support you. Breathe in for a count of five. Hold this breath for the count of five. Breathe out for a count of five. Repeat this for as long as you wish.

When you feel ready, allow your breath to return to its normal rhythm. If you find that your mind begins to wander or you begin thinking of things that cause you to stress, anxiety, or make you feel insecure, come back to your five-count breathing. Focusing on your breath and counting the inhalations, pauses, and exhalations will help remind you of your purpose here.

As you lie here, repeat to yourself, "I am…" This is the mantra for the root chakra. You can complete "I am…" with any additional positive statement you like. Here are some examples:

I am strong
I am curious
I am capable
I am supported
I am worthy
I am enough

During your time in this space, repeat your chosen "I am" statement for as long as you like (or for long as you have time). This is an excellent way to set up the right kind of energy for yourself as you begin your day!

Remember, energy follows focus. When you direct your energy toward the things you want to achieve in your life, you will get there.

This exercise should be done as often as possible, especially when you are working toward a goal. I like to practice this for a few minutes each day after I practice yoga and meditate. This is before I begin bustling around the house to get everyone off to school, and before I take on my workload. It reminds me that I am enough and that I can achieve anything.

A ROOT CHAKRA TEA

This recipe makes roughly 1 and ½ tablespoons of tea blend, which will brew 3-6 cups of tea, depending on how strong you like it and the size of the cup you use. This is an effective morning tea, with a small caffeine boost. The cinnamon creates a subtle sweetness while the ginger provides a little boost of heat.

Ingredients:

- 1 tablespoon (pu-erh or black)
- 1/4 teaspoon cinnamon chips
- 1/8 teaspoon dried ginger (or 1/8 to 1/4 inch fresh root, grated)

Note: If using fresh ginger, I suggest using a small amount and testing the flavor. Adding too much fresh ginger can be *very* strong, and it can easily overwhelm a tea. (After all, good fresh ginger is pungent and spicy, as it should be!)

Directions:

Mix the ingredients together in a small bowl. Place 1 to 1 and ½ teaspoons of the blend in a reusable muslin tea bag or tea ball and place in your cup. (You can also leave the herbs loose in the cup and strain them out with a strainer after brewing.)

Pour 6-8 ounces of boiling water over the herbs. Allow the tea to steep for about 3-5 minutes, depending on your flavor preference. The longer it steeps, the more robust the flavor. Remove the steeped herbs and enjoy!

Ideally, you can enjoy this tea after you perform the root chakra floor exercise discussed above. I find sitting with a sweet and spicy tea helps me come back to reality without losing the purpose or the message of the root chakra exercise.

Chapter Four: SACRAL CHAKRA, SWADHISTHANA

The Sacral Chakra at a glance:

Sanskrit name: Swadhisthana
Governing location: lower abdomen, reproductive organs
Color: orange
Element: Water
Psychological and behavioral functions:
- Sexuality
- Emotions, feelings
- Relationships and relating to others
- Sensual pleasure
- Creativity
- Fantasies

Sacral Chakra Mantra: "I feel…"

"I feel blessed"
"I feel valued"
"I feel energetic"
"I feel love"

Swadhisthana, the sacral chakra, is centered just above the root chakra in the pelvic and lower abdomen area. This is your passion and pleasure center.

While the root chakra governs survival and security, the sacral chakra governs pleasure and enjoyment. This chakra is the experience and expression of our feelings and sensations. It governs behavioral functions related to emotions/feelings within relationships, our ability to relate to others, sensuality and sexuality, sensing the outer and inner worlds, creativity, and indulgence in fantasies.

Swadhisthana is particularly active in our sense of sexuality, sensual pleasure, the physical ability to feel orgasm, and the healthy expression of our sensual and sexual desires. The energy of the sacral chakra allows you to let go, to move, and to feel change and transformation occurring within your body. It enables you to experience this moment as it is, in its fullness. Your ability to let go and feel is essential when it comes to sensing and expressing pleasure, both physical and emotional. When we are unable to allow the flow of energy to move through the body, we can stunt our ability to find pleasure and enjoy life on many levels.

SWADHISTHANA AND WESTERN CULTURE

One main challenge for the second chakra is the conditioning of our society. We live in a culture where feelings are not valued, where passion and emotional reactions are tightly controlled. Furthermore, our emotional expressions are often strongly condemned. Especially as adults, we find ourselves apologizing for emotional expressions related to grief, fear, and anxiety. We tell even those closest to us, "I'm sorry" for crying or getting emotional, even when the occasion deserves an emotional response.

At a very young age, we are often taught to "control ourselves." How many of us have heard throughout our childhoods that "big" girls and boys don't cry or get upset? We are told emotions are invalid or unacceptable. This message has rooted itself profoundly into all we perceive in the world, most notably in corporate and other work environments. Within these tightly controlled and structured environments, the philosophies of "keep it together" and "be professional" are endlessly perpetuated. Men and women alike are tightly regulated on a fundamental level in these places.

From this long-term conditioning, we become disconnected from our bodies, our feelings, and our ability to express. This is evident even in the messaging we've heard throughout the years: "Buck up," "Suck it up," and "Keep a stiff upper lip."

We learn to stifle our emotions, creating a void within. The enforcement of these philosophies creates a lack of emotional freedom, which in turn helps create a lack of empathy for others and for ourselves. We learn to believe that being tough or having "a thick skin" is more important than being human.

Our disconnection from healthy emotional expression is further perpetuated within the social wounds of our culture: through our emotional disconnect, we create a sexual disconnect. Women are told to be sexy and beautiful, but only if they are of a certain age and body type.

Women are directly and indirectly told from childhood that they should look a certain way and behave in a certain way, only to be reprimanded and condemned for it later. Developing a healthy body image as a woman is almost impossible, as mixed and contradictory messages flood into the minds and emotional centers of little girls and women alike.

Men also struggle with the mixed messages of our culture. Perhaps the most damaging in the long term is the one they get beginning at a very young age. "Boys don't cry." The mixed messages our boys and men receive are not only confusing, but they are also often toxic.

Being tender and open clashes with a cultural acceptance of sexual violence and the idea that men must have control or dominate women. Sensuality and sexuality are confused with objectifying the body. The objectification of women's bodies is glorified in the media, yet is condemned at the same time. Mixed signals about what is acceptable and safe create blockages that can prove challenging to clear. But with the right work and in the right amount, blockages *can* be cleared, and the chakra can become balanced.

When your sacral chakra is imbalanced, you will likely feel a great deal of shame, internal pain, and guilt. Passion and love are hard for you to feel and express outwardly to others. You will likely have issues with sexual intimacy. You may also experience emotional instability, fear of change, sexual dysfunction, lack of sexual desire, and addiction. You will likely experience a measurable amount of self-doubt and depression. You may find yourself accepting a false reality created for you through social conditioning. After all, it is the reality you have been groomed to accept.

Women who have an imbalanced sacral chakra may also find their monthly cycles are erratic, as the body expresses the imbalance within. You might find your cycle being non-existent or overly active. Heavy menstrual flow is one common symptom that should be addressed with your doctor, as well as on an energetic level.

JOURNAL THERAPY

The following exercise is meant to help you identify if you have a blocked sacral chakra. Get out your journal and respond to the following questions:

- Do you find it hard to get excited about things that once gave you joy? Does this inability to feel excitement crop up when you should feel excited (i.e., when you achieve something, when something good comes your way, or during a special occasion)?

- Do you find it is difficult to express and sense your emotions? Do you feel cut off from them?

- Do you find yourself having negative associations related to sex, sensuality, and sexuality?

- Do you have difficulty expressing yourself sexually?

- Do you feel you are not worthy of feeling sensual pleasure?

- Do you struggle with your self-image or self-confidence?

- Do you struggle to resolve toxic or non-supportive relationships? Or do you have difficulty recognizing when a relationship is unhealthy or non-supportive?

If you find yourself ready to take a look at your sacral chakra and get it back into balance, it is time to be conscious of your thoughts and internal self-talk. It is time to enjoy the full beauty and benefits of life and all it has to offer. One action you can take in working to heal and balance your sacral chakra is to literally do more of what makes you happy. Ditch negative internal chatter and replace it with joy.

With an open and balanced Swadhisthana chakra, you will have a deepening sense of self-worth, confidence, and ability to grow. You will begin to develop healthy relationships with people who support you and want to help you move forward instead of holding you back in life.

When your second chakra becomes open and balanced, you will likely feel a surge of creativity and the desire to act. You will find it simpler to regain your passion and zest for life, and easier to start and complete projects you have been putting off. You may also see your relationships and the quality of your social networks improve. You will find yourself surrounded by those who love and support you, without having to beg for their support and love.

EXERCISE AND THE SACRAL CHAKRA

Exercise is an essential element when we are seeking to create balance. This applies to all areas. Walking is a great activity you can utilize when you want to balance your lower chakras. Try taking a 30-60-minute walk outside whenever possible. If you can't go out, then walk on a treadmill for a while. You can even incorporate reading something productive and positive while walking. The point is to get the body moving and to help great balance.

When we speak specifically about the sacral chakra, we should also incorporate activities that help us become aware of how our body moves, and how it feels while it is moving. Dancing, especially a sensual form of dancing, is great for helping you gain this awareness. Belly dance is one of the best forms of dance you can utilize when you want to recalibrate your mind with your body. Consider taking a class or watching online videos about belly dancing or even sensual Latin-style dancing. If walking isn't an option, or you just want something new in your routine, try dancing for 30-60 minutes a day instead.

HERBS FOR THE SACRAL CHAKRA

For balancing Swadhisthana chakra, I like to use herbs and plants that are orange in color, and/or support the reproductive system, virility, and hormonal balance. Black cohost, calendula, chamomile, lady's mantle, mint, and raspberries are great examples. For men, horny goat weed is an excellent herb to utilize, while ashwagandha is a great herb for women to incorporate into their daily routine.

The element of water associated with the sacral chakra. Think of how water moves: it is fluid, taking the path of least resistance. It can be soft and tender or robust and passionate. Be sure to drink lots of water and herbal teas as often as you can when working with the element of water, or any time, really. You will also want to eat plenty of fresh fruits that have a high water content, like oranges, melons, strawberries, tangerines, apples, apricots, passion fruit, and grapes.

When we think of the sacral chakra, it's okay to think about the erotic! Plants you might want to incorporate into your diet more often are fleshy fruits like papaya, peaches, and mangos, and vegetables such as squash, carrots, yams, orange peppers, and sweet potatoes. All of these foods are very fragrant, and they taste delicious!

A SIMPLE SACRAL CHAKRA RECIPE

Eating a lot of vegetables, especially orange ones, will help you as you heal and balance your sacral chakra. If you can incorporate herbs in with your vegetables and fruits, you will not only diversify your diet, but you will intensify your healing process. Here is a simple carrot and cucumber salad I find delicious and refreshing.

Ingredients:

- 3 large carrots
- 2 large cucumbers
- 2 green onions, thinly sliced
- 2 tablespoons white wine vinegar
- 2 tablespoons fresh lime juice
- 2 tablespoons extra-virgin olive oil
- 1 teaspoon red pepper flakes
- 1 tablespoon cilantro, finely chopped

- 1 teaspoon sesame seeds, plus more for topping
- Salt and freshly ground black pepper to taste

Directions:

Use a spiralizer to cut the cucumbers and carrots into thin strips, or julienne by hand with a knife. Thinly slice the green onion.

In a medium bowl, whisk together olive oil, vinegar, lime juice, and red pepper flakes. Season with salt and freshly ground black pepper to taste.

In a salad bowl, combine the cilantro, cucumbers, carrots, and green onion. Drizzle the dressing on top, and toss gently.

Top with sesame seeds before serving and enjoy!

Chapter Five: SOLAR PLEXUS CHAKRA, MANIPURA

The Solar Plexus Chakra at a Glance:

Sanskrit name: Manipura
Governing location: navel to the upper torso
Color: yellow
Element: Fire
Psychological and behavioral functions:
- Self-confidence
- Self-motivation
- Courage
- Willpower & self-control
- The ability to speak up for yourself
- Sense of purpose
- Reliability
- Sense of responsibility

Solar Plexus Mantra: "I can…"

"I can heal"
"I can meet challenges"
"I can live with purpose"

"I can create positive habits"

The third chakra, Manipura, or solar plexus chakra, is centered in the upper abdomen, behind the stomach, and up to the breastbone. This chakra governs the digestive system and its associated organs, including the liver, pancreas, gallbladder, and small and large intestines.

Manipura also governs metabolism, blood sugar regulation, and the assimilation of muscles. In the physical body, the solar plexus is a network, or "plexus," of nerves in the pit of the stomach that communicate with the abdominal organs. The nerves themselves are said to resemble rays of the sun meeting together at the center.

The name "Manipura" combines the Sanskrit words for "gem" (*mani*) and "city" (*pura*), and is often translated as "city of jewels." Manipura is our center of personal power, and governs our sense of self-worth and well-being, as well as our personality, our authenticity, our sense of identity and individual freedom, and our ability to make choices. Willpower and motivation are also inherently related to this chakra.

It is said that Manipura is where emotional memories are stored, and many people feel emotion strongly in this part of their body. This is also the place where our "gut feeling" resides. The solar plexus chakra also governs how we perceive and interact with the external world. When balanced, it provides us with the capacity to feel happiness, joy, and a sense of belonging.

A balanced solar plexus will provide you with confidence. This is not to be confused with arrogance or conceit. Real confidence is not ego or fear-driven; instead, it is more about self-support and self-assurance. It is the seat of having a solid belief in yourself, knowing that you will have some level of success in everything you set out to do.

When this chakra is in balance, you will feel self-motivated and have a sense of purpose. You will likely use your personal power to benefit others, rather than trying to control others. The greater good is often at the core of what you set out to achieve.

A balanced solar plexus gives you the capacity to "rise to the occasion" in times of need. This chakra empowers you to follow through and take on the roles or activities many shy away from due to a lack of self-assurance and confidence. It also reminds you to not be distracted from your true path.

MANIPURA OUT OF BALANCE

When the solar plexus is out of balance, it can show in many ways. You may suffer from low self-esteem. You might find it hard to make simple choices, or you may have issues with control. The need for perfectionism can develop, and some will develop OCD behaviors. Imbalances of the solar plexus can often manifest in the physical body. Issues like fatigue, overeating, excessive weight around the stomach, and digestive system disorders such as IBS, ulcers, hypoglycemia, and diabetes could all be a result of an imbalanced chakra.

Those who have an imbalanced solar plexus can also have trouble thinking of others. Some may even develop narcissistic tendencies. Their motivations are purely self-driven out of the desire to show off or establish a sense of superiority over others. Being self-assured turns to arrogance and conceit. A person with an imbalance in this area may still rise to the occasion when the necessity calls for it, but they are no longer acting out of benefiting the whole; instead, they will want recognition, pats on the back, and so on.

My son has a very balanced solar plexus chakra. When I work with him using Reiki, I often ask him to hover his hands over a particular area of my body, and I will sense the energy he is allowing to flow. He is young and has not yet learned to temper his output, and overwhelmingly his solar plexus energy comes through, like lightning in the body. In fact, his energy is so vibrant I often have to ask him to remove his hands or move his hands to another location to avoid feeling nauseous. This is especially evident when he hovers over my solar plexus. The intensity is immediate. We laugh and giggle at my reaction. My son is 10 years old, so of course, he finds this hilarious, which only encourages him to do it more.

HERBS FOR THE SOLAR PLEXUS CHAKRA

There are many herbs we can use to help balance and activate our solar plexus chakra. Here are a few of my favorites: calendula, chamomile, fennel, ginger, goldenrod, lemon, lemon balm, lemongrass, marigold, mint, slippery elm, and turmeric.

EXERCISE AND THE SOLAR PLEXUS CHAKRA

When we engage the body physically, we also help our chakras balance and heal. Breaking out of your typical routine is a great way to revitalize your solar plexus. If you are used to standing all day, try stopping every hour or so and stretch or do some squats. If you sit all day, try to stand up and do something different for a few minutes.

I mentioned in Chapter 2 the idea of installing a treadmill under your desk to create a walking workstation. I did this recently, and I can't tell you how much better I feel. As a writer, I spend *a lot* of time sitting and, well, writing. I found my legs were starting to swell, and my back was hurting. Now I switch between walking and writing and sitting and writing. It creates more balance for my work and lifestyle. It was a simple adjustment to make. But if you're unable to do this, there certainly are other ways you can adjust your behavior to help create more balance.

If you have not made it a habit to walk each day, start taking time out to do so. Try a hike, walk around the block, or walk around your favorite park. Spending time in nature will also help your healing and create balance. Weight training is also another great exercise you should consider incorporating. When our bodies feel resilient, our confidence is automatically boosted. Try using small weights, and after a few weeks increase the weight a little, just be careful not to overdo it.

SOLAR PLEXUS CHAKRA HERBAL BATH

Often when we think of tea, we only think of drinking tea. In my line of work, I make teas for a variety of purposes, including bathing. Tea can also be used to wash your walls and floors, especially when we are working with energy. I enjoy using baths to soothe and balance the solar plexus because of the element of water. The solar plexus, when imbalanced, can be very fiery and overwhelming. Using water and herbs to soothe and balance this chakra works well.

Keep in mind that this will also work in the shower. You can bundle the herbs up in cheesecloth with twine or string and and sponge the tea over your body, or tie them under your shower head, allowing the water to filter through the herbs.

Ingredients:

These herbs and flowers can be fresh or dried. I measure my teas in parts so I can make a smaller or larger amount as needed.

- 1 part lemon balm leaves
- 1 part dandelion flowers
- ½ part marigold flowers
- ½ part lemon peel
- ½ part chamomile flowers
- ¼ part ginger root, sliced
- Cheese cloths & twine or string
- 1/2 to 1 Gallon of water

Directions:

Begin with a large pot of fresh water on the stove. Place all your herbs in the water and bring them to a boil. Reduce the heat and allow them to simmer for about 2 minutes and remove from the heat. Cover your tea and allow it to sit for an additional 10 minutes.

Bathtub Method: If you are soaking in this tea, you will need to strain the plants from your tea as you pour it into your tub water. Cheesecloth or a fine mesh strainer is ideal for this process. If using cheesecloth, you can also make an herb bundle to place in the water as you soak.

Before you soak in your tea, think of one area in your life that makes you feel like you are unable or where you lack confidence. Take this situation and the feelings it brings up with you into the bathroom and into the tub as you soak. Draw your bath as warm as you like it, add your tea to the water, and get in. Soak in this mixture for as long as you like.

As you soak, envision your yellow glowing solar plexus rotating in a smooth clockwise motion. You can see it as a ball of yellow light or a many-petaled flower, like a dandelion or daisy. Feel the herbs seeping into your pores as you relax and allow yourself to feel balanced.

If at any time you sense or realize your thoughts have turned negative or judgmental, imagine a glowing yellow light around your body, and allow this light to gently cleanse away these feelings, thoughts, and negativities. Feel the blockages and limiting beliefs you once carried with you being soothed away. Allow the herbs to soften your skin and revitalize your body, continuing to envision your solar plexus rotating clockwise until you feel finished with the bath.

When you get out, towel off and sit for a moment in the peace and balance you have created for yourself. Allow any additional disparaging thoughts to fall away from you and into the tub water. As you drain the tub, imagine all the blockages and limitations you cleansed from your energy field draining out with the water from the bath.

Shower Method: In the shower, we can modify this technique to work without having to soak. In this version, you will want to use cheesecloth to create an herb bundle that can be easily removed from the pot before heading to the shower.

Simply place your herbs into the cheesecloth and tie the herbs up. This bundle will then be removed from the pot after steeping and tied under your shower head, where the water from your shower can filter through the remaining herbs. Here is how I do it:

1. Prepare your shower. You will want to have a large sponge or washcloth with you.

2. Place your herbs in the cheesecloth on the shower head. If you make a large loop with your string or twine, you can simply slip it over your shower head, making it easy to remove later.

3. Once you are ready and you have your items in a place you can get into your shower

4. Now set your intention. Think of one area in your life that makes you feel like you are unable or where you lack confidence. Take this situation and the

feelings it brings up with you and step into your shower.

Once you are in, you will allow the water to filter through the herbs you placed on your shower head and begin envisioning your yellow solar plexus rotating in a clockwise motion. You can see it as a ball of yellow light or a many-petaled flower, like a dandelion or daisy. Next, begin to gather the tea with your sponge or washcloth and bathe your body with the herbal mixture.

If at any time you sense or realize your thoughts have turned negative or judgmental, imagine a glowing yellow light around your body, and allow this light to gently cleanse away these feelings, thoughts, and negativities. Feel the energy of the plants seep into your pores and allow the blend to soften your skin and revitalize your body. Remain here in this activity as long as you feel necessary.

When you are done, squeeze out any remaining tea down the drain, turn off the shower, and towel off. Sit for a moment, feeling the soothing yellow light of your solar plexus vibrating and shining bright yellow. If you discover any additional disparaging thoughts popping up in your head, you can send them down the drain with your water.

When you are ready, you should bury or compost your left-over herbs. Ideally, if you have a garden or potted plant, you can place them in the soil. This allows the herbs to work on a physical level to nourish the plant, which also allows their energetic function to transmute old negativity into something positive.

Chapter Six:
HEART CHAKRA, ANAHATA

The Heart Chakra at a Glance:

Sanskrit name: Anahata
Governing location: heart, shoulders, arms
Color: green
Element: Air
Psychological and behavioral functions:
- Unconditional love
- Self-love
- Self-care
- Compassion/empathy
- Connectedness

Heart Chakra Mantra: "I love..."

"I love life"
"I love myself"
"I am loved"
"I am love"

Anahata, or heart chakra, is the unification chakra in between the upper and lower chakras. As we have learned so far, each chakra is connected. When one chakra is imbalanced, it is often assisted by another. As we work through the mid and upper chakras throughout the rest of this book, you will notice more and more that the chakras "bleed" more easily into one another.

Often referred to as the "Bridge Chakra," Anahata is the center of the chakra system. It is the central powerhouse of the subtle (or luminous) body discussed in Chapter 1. We call the heart chakra the "bridge" because it is the connection between the luminous body and the physical body, and between Heaven and Earth, or the ethereal and physical realms. It helps us keep perspective when we have one foot in the physical world and one in the Otherworld.

The heart chakra plays a critical role in your spiritual and physical experiences and development. Many, if not most spiritual traditions, recognize love as the ultimate healing and unifying force. This is prominently reflected in Anahata. It is working to bring balance to your physical and spiritual self by allowing you to know your physical self as well as your spiritual self.

The heart chakra is associated with unconditional love, empathy, sympathy, and enjoyment. This is your wellspring of love, warmth, compassion, and happiness. Anahata moves love through your life. It also helps you experience life with a sense of gratitude and belonging.

This chakra anchors your sense of compassion toward yourself and others and helps you develop deep bonds with all living things. It helps influence your sense of kindness towards others, and your feelings of self-love, altruism, generosity, and empathy. In the process, the heart also oversees and helps develop your understanding of respect for yourself and others.

When the heart chakra is open and balanced, you are better able to recognize and appreciate that we are all part of something greater. You can see or sense your interconnectedness with all living things and the universe. You can better understand the importance of all relationships, from simple friendships to the intricacies of the universe and the complexities of ecosystems and life cycles here on earth. The heart chakra helps us recognize that there are a fundamental truth and necessity in the seemingly random patterns of nature.

When the heart chakra is balanced and healthy, we live our lives in loving-kindness and show compassion towards others. Through your display of compassion and kindness, you will inspire the same qualities in others. You are also able to recognize and more readily come to terms with the ups and downs we experience as humans. In this capacity, we can see through a more transparent lens of what it means to be human. Through this lens, you can see that all things are temporary. Trauma can be healed. Neglect can be rectified. Sadness can be alleviated, and deprivation can be replaced with abundance.

The heart chakra is the source of profound truths that cannot be articulated in words. The heart is the mediator between body and spirit, and it directly influences vitality and balance. Like air entering the lungs and dispersing within the body, the heart chakra integrates a spiritual understanding of love, compassion, and connection to everything you encounter.

Love, like air, is within and all around. When we can recognize its presence, the reality becomes profound. The intangible becomes tangible. You will feel connected to the world around you on many levels, allowing you to recognize and understand it. I also find it becomes easier to translate the intangibility of love (like air) to others in a more literal and coherent capacity.

ANAHATA OUT OF BALANCE

Deficiencies and imbalances in the heart chakra can affect your overall well-being. Mentally and emotionally, an imbalanced heart chakra can result in challenging issues, such as co-dependence, manipulative behaviors, feeling unworthy, or having the inability to trust yourself or others. Self-love will be sacrificed due to the belief that you are somehow undeserving.

When the imbalance is allowed to continue, you will likely begin to believe that self-care is not necessary or that it is a waste of time. There may even come a time when you convince yourself that it is selfish to take time out for yourself, further perpetuating the cycle of imbalance.

When the heart chakra needs healing, you may also experience an excessive need to isolate yourself, as you withdraw from social engagements, activities, and more. This is often due to a lack of empathy for yourself or others. You might find interacting with others difficult or unpleasant because you end up judging yourself and others when triggered.

Further blockages and imbalances can leave you with a sense of numbness toward most events, people, and expressions. You can feel unworthy of love, or you may feel like you have no love to give. You are mostly closed off from yourself and others. If you feel this is the case for yourself, it is essential to gain a sense of compassion and empathy toward others. You will need to do the work to open and balance your heart chakra, which will likely also help stabilize you as a whole.

Closures and imbalances can become reinforced through years of being unable to express ourselves without judgment and ridicule from others. As a result, you may also experience the inability to forgive others or move on from negative experiences. Sometimes the issue can become so impairing that even minor incidents can cause you to mull the issue over and over in your head.

You may find yourself revisiting the details in the shower or before you fall asleep at night. In rehashing prior encounters with 'I should have said this…", or 'I should have done that…", you are further enforcing the present blockage. In this case, a solid dose of self-love is vital for healing. Instead of judging yourself or criticizing your actions or inactions, try cutting yourself a break and remind yourself you did the best you could at the time. Take the opportunity to remind yourself that you are learning and growing each day.

Additional signs that you have a blocked or imbalanced heart chakra, can show up as you become more critical of yourself and others. The idea that you are a perpetual victim seems to also reoccur. When we are not at peace with ourselves, it becomes increasingly difficult to come to terms with the importance of forgiveness. One step toward balance is loving yourself enough to forgive yourself for any hurt you may have caused. This applies to the hurt you cause yourself. Once this has happened, you can then seek forgiveness from those whom you have hurt.

Other symptoms of an imbalanced heart chakra may manifest in a lack of good judgment in relationships. You may find that you are running from one toxic, unproductive, abusive, or disruptive relationship to another. This pattern will leave you emotionally drained and sometimes unable to see the pattern(s) you follow.

Some might also feel the need to overexert themselves in relationships, allowing relationships to become overly demanding. This is often most noted in women as we tend to take on the demands of others more readily. In this case, the relationship becomes overly dependent on one person, expecting this person to give a hundred and ten percent, one hundred percent of the time. This leaves the person holding all the demands and responsibilities.

You may also feel ruled by your emotions and unable to make wise or rational choices for yourself. With an imbalanced heart chakra, you can become codependent or entirely dependent on others, expecting them to initiate all the necessary elements within a relationship, like intimacy or primary bonding. You can also experience a loss of personal identity and a lack of personal boundaries. You can begin to think or believe that to gain love or feel loved by others, you need to give in or say "Yes" to every demand or request. Eventually, this pattern will drain you and leave you completely unable to care for yourself.

In addition to these social and emotional issues, when our Anahata is blocked and imbalanced, we may experience physical misalignments or disease. Poor circulation, high or low blood pressure, or heart and lung conditions can result. The heart chakra directly affects the upper back, upper torso, heart, lungs, chest, arms, and hands. This chakra governs the function of flow, or circulation, of air and blood within the physical body, and energy within the luminous body.

JOURNAL THERAPY

How do you love yourself? Using what you've learned so far, journal your thoughts. This is a great journaling exercise you can use to sift through your feelings, experiences, and beliefs around what is happening in the world today, as well as how you show up in the world. Take time to reflect on these questions.

- Do you feel imbalanced with your heart chakra?

- What areas do you identify in your life and habits that might give you a clue?

- How can you show someone you love how much you admire and adore them? How can you do the same for yourself?

HERBS FOR THE HEART CHAKRA

Angelica, astragalus, elecampane, ginger, hawthorn, hibiscus, hops, lady's mantle, lotus petals, marjoram, motherwort, mullein, nettle, passionflower, sweet Annie, tulsi, rose, and violets are great herbs to use for the heart chakra. Mullein in particular is excellent for softening, especially the skin. It is also burned as an incense or drunk as a tea to help heal and support lung health.

TEA AND CEREMONY FOR THE HEART CHAKRA

Green tea is an excellent base for making tea blends to help you open and balance your heart chakra. I prefer Imperial Green Tea, which has a lighter flavor than other types of green tea (such as gunpowder) and works great when blending in other herbs, fruits, and roots.

For this ceremony, you will want to set up a place for yourself where you can sit in relative silence and will not be disturbed for a few minutes. We will be engaging all the lower chakras as we heal and balance the heart, and you will need space and the ability to focus while you do this.

Not everyone has a whole room to dedicate to self-care, mediation, and quiet rituals, but even if all you have is a closet, you can clear it out and use it as your space when you need it. You can also perform this outside if you prefer.

Tools:

- Kettle or pot for boiling water
- Teacup
- Fine mesh strainer, tea ball, or reusable muslin tea bag
- Pillows, blankets, cushions, etc. as desired
- Soft music (optional)
- Candles (optional)
- Incense (optional)

Ingredients:

- 1 part Imperial Green Tea (or other green tea of your choice)
- ½ part nettle
- ¼ part hibiscus
- ¼ part rose petals

Blend the herbs together and use about 1-1 and 1/2 teaspoons per 6-8 oz of water. Steep for 3-5 minutes or until it reaches your desired flavor preference.

The Ritual:

Put water on to boil for the tea. While the water heats, set yourself up where you feel most comfortable. You will want to be at ease and feel secure as you experience this small ritual.

I like to make a sort of nest with pillows on the floor with a tray for my tea, so I can remove the herbs from the steeped tea during the ritual—bring a second cup (if pouring through a strainer) or other receptacle to place the herbs on once you remove them.

Pour the water and bring your tea to your sitting space. Focus on the sensations of sitting quietly and caring for yourself. Focus on the comfort of the pillows and the chair or sofa that supports you. (If you're on the floor, feel how the floor supports you.) As the tea brews, watch as the water changes color. See this as a conscious act between the element of earth and water. When allowed, the two become so in love with each other, they create something new together. Feel how your hands support the cup as you bring the tea to your lips for a sip.

Remove the herbs when the tea is at the strength you prefer. As you drink your tea, reflect on the feeling within the center of your chest. Feel how the tea warms your chest as you drink it.

Take your time here. Sip your tea and allow the compassion of earth and water to fill your body and spirit—all the work of mother nature, here to nurture you at this moment.

Chapter Seven:
THROAT CHAKRA, VISHUDDHA

The Throat Chakra at a Glance:

Sanskrit name: Vishuddha
Governing location: throat, neck, head (up to the eyes)
Color: blue
Element: Akasha/Ether
Psychological and behavioral functions:
- Self-expression
- Speaking your truth
- Speaking clearly
- Able to convey your needs to others
- Integrity
- Innovation
- Authenticity

Throat Chakra Mantra: "I express…"

"I express my truth"
"I express with love"
"I express clearly"
"I express my soul"

Located in the region of the neck, the throat chakra, or Vishuddha, is the fifth chakra within our seven-chakra system. Vishuddha is the first of the three higher or upper chakras on the "chakra ladder." With a secure connection to your sacral chakra and solar plexus chakras, your throat chakra embodies your innovation and authenticity. The Sanskrit name translates to "especially pure," an appropriate name for this chakra, as the throat chakra is associated with speaking your authenticity.

Vishuddha is responsible for communicating effectively and with conviction. This is not to be confused with combative or aggressive forms of expression. The expression embodied by Vishuddha is reflective of the heart chakra. Motivated through the expression of truth, the throat chakra allows us to speak through the heart, using the solar and sacral chakras as our guides. This is a good example of the importance of having a well-balanced and maintained chakra system, as each one affects the others.

As the center of communication and creativity, the throat chakra allows us to express who we are. When your fifth chakra's energy is in harmony, you will stand up for what you believe in, be honest with yourself (and others), and speak your truth without apprehension. Vishuddha also gives us the capacity to learn how to listen deeply to others.

When your throat chakra is balanced, you will feel inspired to act on projects and ideas. This action will also be led by your solar plexus. As you work toward your goals and aspirations, you will also have the ability to align your vision while being realistic about what you cannot achieve. When balanced, you will achieve great things for the benefit of yourself and those around you.

VISHUDDHA OUT OF BALANCE

The power of the throat chakra starts in the center of the neck at your throat or vocal cords and expands upward to your mouth. It also radiates to the back of the neck and down to the shoulders. You can sense or notice if your throat chakra is imbalanced by seeing how your body reacts when you speak your truth to others. If you find, when you speak your truth, that your shoulders hunch or draw up to your ears and your neck tenses, chances are your throat chakra is not healthy and balanced. It's also safe to speculate that your solar and sacral chakras need some work.

An underactive throat chakra can contribute to feelings of insecurity, nervousness, and introversion. You may feel terrified when the need to speak up for yourself arises. When the throat chakra becomes blocked, a detachment from your authenticity is often present. You may feel insecure and unwanted. You fear speaking up for your needs, desires, and pain because you don't feel valued or that your needs are important enough to be expressed.

You may find yourself speaking the truth or bringing an issue into the light and later saying, "I shouldn't have opened my big mouth!" This kind of internal self-talk only feeds feelings of being timid, and unable to speak up against dangerous behaviors or injustices. This also maintains an imbalance within the Vishuddha and connected chakras. You become your worst critic, over-analyzing every word. You may reach a point where you no longer speak unless it's necessary for getting your basic needs met.

When I think of the issues an imbalanced chakra system can cause, I think of Maya Angelou and her experience as a young girl in speaking up for herself. According to Marcia Ann Gillespie's biography of Angelou, at the age of eight, Maya was raped and abused by her mother's boyfriend. Maya told her brother about what happened, and he later told the rest of their family. Freeman was found guilty in court, but was jailed for only one day. Four days after his release, Freeman was killed. It is believed he was killed by Angelou's uncles. Maya became mute for about five years after this. "I thought, *my voice killed him; I killed that man because I told his name*," said Angelou. "And then I thought I would never speak again because my voice would kill anyone."

Through this trauma, Angelou believed that her voice was the issue, and there was no source of support to tell her otherwise. In her world, she was wrong, instead of the man who harmed her. She was just a child, and the beliefs we hold as children can often have profound effects on us throughout life. Later, Maya was able to heal and speak her truth, becoming one of the most prolific female black writers and poets of our country. To this day, she is one of my most cherished role models.

The imbalance of your throat chakra may also swing the other way. You may find your mouth or your need to speak goes into overdrive. If your throat chakra is overactive, you may be experiencing a lack of control over your speech. You may have trouble getting the words out or find that you are talking too much. You may also speak without a filter, unable to recognize when your words are harmful, judgmental, or disparaging.

In this state, you may openly express that you are speaking your truth, when in actuality, this is a defense mechanism. In a state of overwhelm, an imbalance like this can lead to you become a harsh vocal critic of yourself and others. You may experience struggles in your relationships because your form of communication is often combative, argumentative, or overly critical towards others.

You may also find that you inadvertently or unconsciously gossip about others. An imbalanced throat chakra can cause us to speak with arrogance and conceit, with a rude or condescending tone. You may also have trouble listening to others. You might listen but only for the purpose of an argument or rebuttal. You might feel an overwhelming need to express your point of view or collection of knowledge, even if it is not helpful in the current situation. In this state, you are overwhelmed with the need to speak and be heard, making authentic active listening very difficult.

Within the body, the throat chakra governs the thyroid, vocal cords, neck, and shoulders. This chakra also influences the health of your teeth, gums, arms, and hands. Hypothyroidism appears to be shared in those who have a blocked or underactive throat chakra. You may also experience frequent mouth ulcers and similar sores (mouth herpes), sore throat/tonsillitis, gingivitis, TMJ, and tension in the neck and shoulders. Women seem to be especially affected by this imbalance.

JOURNAL THERAPY

Journaling is an excellent way to regain your ability to express yourself. Sometimes I sit with my journal and write 2-3 pages of whatever comes to my mind. No matter if it is sensitive or incomprehensible. I just write what my brain and emotions produce, and I practice expressing myself through words using my journal.

In this exercise, reflect on a time when you refrained from speaking up when someone did something wrong. Reflect on how their actions made you feel. Reflect on how their actions affected other people. Finally, reflect on how you felt after allowing them to get away with their actions and remaining silent. Allow your feelings to bubble and become present. Again, as in all journaling, this is not a time to judge yourself. This is a time for acknowledgement. Simply allow the truth to become clear.

Once you write down your experience, put this entry away for a while and then come back to it. Take some additional time to see how this experience feels. Do you need additional healing and forgiveness in this situation? How can you be gentle with yourself, and understand that you did the best you could within your capacity at the time?

HERBS FOR THE THROAT CHAKRAS

Blackberries, blueberries, cabbage (purple or red), currants, elderberries, ginger root, grapes, licorice root, mallow, olives (black), plums, raisins, and slippery elm bark are great options when working with this chakra. Cutting out added sugar can also be beneficial to the throat.

CLEARING YOUR THROAT TEA

The act of caring for your throat can help you work toward healing your throat chakra, especially when done in a mindful capacity filled with awareness. This is an excellent tea to drink when you are journaling in support of your throat chakra. This tea will also help soothe irritated, swollen, and sore throats.

For one cup of tea, use about 1-1 and ½ teaspoons total of the herbs. You can also make a larger quantity of the blend to have on hand for future use.

Ingredients:

- 1 part mint
- ½ part raspberry leaves
- ¼ part mallow

Instructions:

Blend the herbs together and use about 1-1 and ½ teaspoons per 6-8oz of water.

Steep for 3-5 minutes or until it reaches your desired flavor preference.

VOCAL EXERCISES FOR CLEARING AND CLAIMING YOUR VOICE

What better way to connect with and balance your throat chakra than to use your voice? Take time each day to perform one or more of the following voice activities:

- Go outside and scream. Scream at the sky, the clouds, the air, or nothing at all. Just raise your voice and be heard at the top of your lungs.

- Hum softly to yourself. This exercise teaches the ability to be subtle while being heard. Hum one of your favorite songs to yourself, or a melody from your childhood.

- Sing to yourself. Who cares if you can't carry a tune? That is not the point of this exercise. Sing and sing proudly.

- Speak to yourself. When we hear the sound of our own voice, something impressive seems to happen. This is especially true when we are working through severe issues. When we speak to ourselves about what's on our mind, we can process the information more thoroughly. This allows us to come up with solutions that we might not have recognized otherwise. It's also good for those who don't like writing in a journal—you can use a phone app or recorder of some sort to record your thoughts and experiences.

Chapter Eight:
THIRD EYE CHAKRA, AJNA

The Third Eye Chakra at a Glance:

Sanskrit name: Ajna
Governing location: middle of the eyebrows, forehead, and head
Color: purple or indigo
Element: Light
　Psychological and behavioral functions:
- Intuition
- Perception
- Wisdom
- Inspiration
- Creativity
- Psychic ability/awareness

Third Eye Chakra Mantra: "I receive..."

"I receive guidance"
"I receive blessings"
"I receive positive energy"
"I recieve knowing from my higher self"

Located in the middle of your forehead slightly above the level of your brow, the third eye chakra, or Ajna, is the sixth chakra in our seven-chakra system. "Ajna" translates to mean "perceiving" or "command." This is a fitting name, since the third eye chakra is responsible for how you perceive the world and how you manage your place in it.

Ajna is motivated by intuition, knowledge, introspection, and reflection. It is responsible for the link between your mind, body, and spirit. The energy of this chakra resonates from in-between your brows, just above the bridge of your nose and outward into your body.

The third eye chakra is associated with the other dimensions, or the realm of spirits. It embodies your ability to see both the inner and outer worlds as they exist simultaneously. This is how the connection to the spirit realm, or Otherworld, is made. Through recognizing this connection, we become aware and able to experience clarity of thought and deep self-reflection.

The third eye chakra enables us to use our intuitive sense to recognize, perceive, and translate subtle energies. These energies are all around us, from the aura we might sense around other people to the spirit and the essences within plants. Ajna brings us face to face with the indescribable, or the feelings and sensations we pick up on.

Through our third eye, we become more familiar with the intangible, as it connects us to a different way of seeing and observing. When we utilize the power and benefits of the third eye chakra, we are removed from the perceptions we accumulate and refine through spending a lifetime in the physical world.

When balanced and open, Ajna allows us to peer through the veil to experience the world through energetic sensation, rather than physical cues. Often these sensations, inklings, hunches, or even warnings cannot be fully articulated. Therefore, in many cases, these messages or clues can only be fully understood by the individual receiving the message or information. The visions and pieces of information received through the third eye are often subtle and obscure. They may appear distorted, ghost-like, or dream-like.

When working with the upper chakras, we begin to realize that there is a fine line between sanity, or remaining coherent in the "real" world, and slipping entirely into the spirit realm. Sustaining awareness and balance of third eye chakra energy requires focused practice and attention, just as the regular practice of meditation brings us to a new understanding and perception. Because we have come to learn that balance is critical, we can see that having a balanced chakra system will help us keep one foot in reality and one foot in the spirit realm, without losing our connection entirely to one or the other.

Acquiring the ability to relax into a deep meditation or trance-like state will help establish a stable connection with Ajna. When we focus our mind and awareness, we can move beyond trivial distractions and the illusions placed in our thought patterns through social conditioning and other influences. Here is where we become expansive, void of ego, and the fears ego brings to the table.

Ego can often create a barrier between you and clearer insight. When the barrier is resolved, you can live and create more deeply, and in alignment with your highest good. In this state, we learn to solve our knee-jerk or subconscious reactions, and any reactions led by fear. We establish coherence between the physical world and the spirit realm when we are living authentically.

We also learn to allow self-reflection to become constructive instead of filled with criticism. In this state, we learn to observe our actions, reactions, and attitudes within the moment. We can more readily recognize what best serves our growth as we develop a greater understanding. The pattern of harsh self-criticism becomes resolved. Through this resolution, we become free from depressions induced by judgment. Instead, we can see something bigger at work, and we can recognize that we are part of it.

When balanced, Ajna helps you create a deeper connection to self, your inner-wisdom, and comprehensive insight. This is where you can access your higher-self or inner power for guidance. Knowledge gained and understood through Anja comes deep from within your being where you are connected to universal knowledge. When enabled, you can move past illusion as you access profound truths and infinite knowledge. This is also where we begin to see similarities between the third eye and crown chakras. The two chakras seem to work very closely with one another.

A balanced third eye chakra gives you the ability to be mindful as you learn to live in the present. As your center of wisdom and knowledge, Ajna allows you to open your mind to more in-depth considerations. Everything around you becomes more than what is shown at face value.

When the third eye is in balance, you can learn how to not take things for granted. In working with Ajna, you quickly learn that even the things or experiences you once thought were simple, in fact, have many facets or layers for consideration. When active and balanced, you can better sense the subtle energies and influences that would otherwise be dismissed or go un-noticed. This is where your intuition becomes instrumental. You will gain an increased and acute ability to perceive the subtle nuances of reality, both physical and ethereal.

Through self-reflection, the third eye chakra becomes pivotal in your ability to introspect on your healing, existence, and presence in the world. Through experiencing the intangible, your link between your intuition and the physical world becomes tangible. What seemed obscure and foggy through traditional perception becomes clear and easily understood. This connection allows you to internalize the outer world while you observe and reflect. In this state, logic and creativity may intensify as you gain the ability to utilize your creativity and logical thinking in a balanced and productive way.

AJNA OUT OF BALANCE

An imbalanced Ajna can negatively affect your ability to concentrate or process information. You may have trouble activating and utilizing your intuition. You might live in a constant or chronic state of worry or regret. Fear of the unknown can end up ruling your life as you try to navigate your routine.

You may have developed a habit of not keeping your cool under pressure. You may tend to feel like your world is falling apart over temporary inconveniences or upsets. You may try to compensate by tightly controlling yourself and your environments. When the unexpected does occur, you may find yourself losing all control or, at minimum, experiencing bouts of extreme anxiety. The idea that one might "come unhinged" is a suitable metaphor.

In a state of third eye chakra imbalance, you become unable to recognize the illusions you currently harbor, the same illusions that hold you back. We humans are very good at convincing ourselves that we are who we are and that this will never change.

We are also very good at becoming blind to the contrary or counterproductive habits and traits we maintain, even when they are disruptive and destructive to our well-being and livelihood—if the habit or trait serves a purpose on some level, we continue. We tend to become very good at convincing ourselves that it's not our fault or problem. This mindset is highly toxic and damaging to the balance required for enlightenment and spiritual understanding.

Third eye chakra imbalances can stunt your ability to self-reflect in a healthy and balanced way. Self-criticism and harsh self-talk related to how you should have handled situations may become too painful, making this type of reflection impossible to endure. You may be unable to reflect without criticism and taking on a victim mentality, or you may believe that you can't reflect without using judgment.

When your third eye is imbalanced, you may also feel disconnected or alienated from the spirit and the universe. Perhaps you feel like God has forsaken you or left you. Or maybe to you, God or the Divine does not exist. You may have become overly grounded in the physical, like burying your feet in thick mud. Remaining too grounded in "reality," you will lack the ability to trust the Divine. Therefore, you will remain disconnected from its guidance and power. This will disrupt and block your psychic abilities, or your ability to see with your third eye.

Impulse control may also be an issue when your third eye is off balance. Anything we do in excess can lead to additional feelings of overwhelm. You may experience overindulgences where you are unable to do certain things in moderation. You may also find that you do most things in excess when the slightest disruption to your day occurs. This may include excessive daydreaming, sleeping, or avoidance related to exercising, eating, drinking, etc.

Say you overeat because you had one unfortunate incident at work. Then, because you overate, you punish yourself mentally because you now feel awful about having eaten that entire bag of chips. In retrospect, you see the issue was fleeting or temporary, and you did not need to send yourself over the edge, but with this realization, you punish yourself further. Through this cycle, you will feel mentally and emotionally exhausted.

Another symptom of an imbalanced or blocked third eye is indecisiveness or poor judgment. You may find it impossible to decide on something as simple as what you want to eat for dinner or what color shirt to wear. You may find too many factors running through your head, disrupting your ability to tap into the confidence to know what you want when you want it, at the time when you need it.

When the third eye chakra is off balance, we can become overly analytical and too literal. Not only does this affect good judgment, but it also can lead to issues with being judgmental. In this state of imbalance, we can judge ourselves and others a little too harshly. We can forget the difference between strict judgment and wise discernment, making everything black or white with zero grey to even things out.

When we judge ourselves and others too often, and to the extreme, we will eventually develop anxiety related to everything we do and say. We will become fearful of doing something wrong, making the wrong choice, or saying the wrong thing. By default, we do not like to be judged, but when spending too much time in the state of judgment, we perpetuate the issue.

The third eye chakra governs the brain, eyes, brain function, nose, and the nervous system. When we experience imbalances in this chakra, we will also experience imbalances in these areas. You may have enough of a disruption that you receive a diagnosis of ADD, ADHD, ODD, OCD, or the like. Strokes, blindness, headaches, and other issues related to the brain, eyes, and nose can occur. Perhaps you are accustomed to getting sinus infections, and there has never been a solid reason why. Maybe it is time to work toward balancing this chakra and see if your chronic symptoms improve.

METHODS OF OPENING AND BALANCING YOUR THIRD EYE CHAKRA

Your chakras are in constant fluctuation. Practicing chakra healing, balancing, and aligning is a regular and even daily opportunity you can provide for yourself that will bring you into a better state of balance. Here are a few activities you can try:

Get Outside. This seems to be a recurring suggestion, but nature is a powerful healer. Our connection to nature is something we often forget or dismiss in our current culture. Practice going outside and feeling your connection to the earth, plants, bugs, and animals around you. Try taking a hike to a place where you can see your town or a body of water from a distance. Sit on the earth and feel her support under you. Breath in fresh sun-kissed air. Hug a tree, or do some gardening. Take some time to sit in nature and meditate on your place on the earth. Take this time to be grateful for all the earth provides, from food and oxygen to water and beautiful flowers. Take in the fresh air and watch as the wind sways the grass and leaves on the trees. Allow yourself to become part of the landscape as you become part of it in silent reflection.

Meditation. Since the third eye chakra is also linked to our connection with the Divine, meditation seems like a sound practice. When we learn to create stillness in our minds and lives, we open ourselves to receiving. When balanced, we can more easily receive love, gratitude, peace, and understanding. Messages from the Divine are also more likely to come through as we choose becoming present over living reactively.

Journal Therapy. Once again, journaling is an essential act for healing and balancing our thoughts and emotions, as well as an invaluable tool for processing our thoughts. To work with the third eye chakra, journal about the things you hold on to in this existence. List all the earthly and materialistic 'needs' you might perceive. Maybe you have an overwhelming feeling that you need more of a specific object, like shoes or clothes. Write down the objects you hold on to, and why you feel the need to keep them in your life. Then, highlight the ones that seem to hold you back. If they are linked to an emotion or past experience, ask yourself whether this a positive or negative influence. Does the connection help or hinder you?

Release Ceremony. Is anything holding you back? In the journal exercise above, you had the opportunity to identify the influences, mindsets, and habits related to possessions that no longer serve you. When you've identified which things hold you back and why, try listing the associated thoughts, mindsets, and/or habits down on a separate piece of paper. Next, burn the paper as you let go of these connections. Through the use of ritual, we can learn to let go, heal, and become balanced.

Get Physical. Yoga and the chakras are eternally linked. Since the chakras and yoga are from the same ancient spiritual teachings, yoga is an essential means for bringing your third eye chakra into a place of balanced wellness. Try incorporating a simple yoga practice into your routine. This will help you reinstate your sense of flexibility, resilience, strength, and balance. Many yoga practices directly address the chakras. You can try incorporating these into your routine as well.

Make a choice and stick with it. This can be with regard to meal planning, schedules, or the color shirt you will wear today. If you're struggling with too many daily decisions, take some time each week to plan and place some structure within your routine. For example, make a list of the foods you prefer to eat and plan out some meals. This can help you gain confidence when making decisions, and build your trust in this process.

HERBS FOR THE THIRD EYE CHAKRA

Bilberry, chamomile, dill, eyebright, ginkgo biloba, gotu kola, juniper, lavender, lemon balm, mugwort, poppy, rosemary, star anise, thyme, and valerian all support the third eye chakra.

When made into teas, herbs that act as a sedative or nervine, like chamomile, valerian, and lemon balm, will help ease anxieties. Teas blended to promote cognition, with ingredients like gotu kola and ginkgo biloba, will help you think more clearly.

Chapter Nine:
CROWN CHAKRA, SAHASRARA

The Crown Chakra at a Glance:

Sanskrit name: Sahasrara
Governing location: top of head, and just above the head
Color: white or violet and gold
Element: Intelligence
Psychological and behavioral functions:
- Divine connection
- Sense of unity
- Trust in the Divine
- Sense of being part of something bigger

Crown Chakra Mantra: "I know…"

"I know my intuition"
"I know I am guided"
"I know I am whole"
"I know I am sovereign"

Sahasrara, or crown chakra, is the final chakra within the seven-chakra system. The energy of the crown chakra is seated on the top of your head, like a crown, as the name suggests. Its energy radiates upward and outward, then down through the other chakras in the body. Like the third eye chakra, Sahasrara helps regulate the central nervous system and brain. It also helps govern the muscular and skeletal system. The skin, our largest organ, also falls under this chakra.

Sahasrara is said to be the place where our individual consciousness connects with Divine universal consciousness. This enables you to experience esoteric knowledge, or Divine knowledge. It helps you gain spiritual growth and serves as your connection to the universe. The Sanskrit name, Sahasrara, translates to mean "a thousand petals" because it tends to be viewed in the form of a lotus with 1,000 petals. You can also think of it as a flower crown, where each point of the crown is the tip of a flower reaching to the sky.

Like the third eye, the crown chakra is responsible for transcending your limitations, emotionally, spiritually, physically, and mentally. When you immerse yourself in the energy of your seventh chakra, you find yourself in a state of oneness with the universe. The crown chakra allows you to move beyond the greedy mindsets of the material world, allowing you to connect with the universe as your spirit is allowed to soar to its intended heights. This chakra will enable you to access pure clarity and enlightened wisdom.

The crown chakra is where the physical body and the universe and soul connect and where the conduit for the Divine is open. This chakra embraces gratitude. Gratitude for life, spirit, and the experiences that come in between. This chakra is the seat of enlightenment through attentive consciousness.

When the crown chakra is healthy and balanced, it enables you to experience and perceive serenity and joy, with a deep peace. The raw essence of life becomes available to us on a more physical level. Our senses also awaken, fully allowing us to experience all life has to offer.

Through this enlightened awareness, we become keenly aware that everything is connected, and that our actions and habits are not exclusively experienced by us. We can more clearly see how we influence others. If we choose to engage in harmful or destructive behaviors, we become acutely aware of our harmful or destructive impact.

If we decide to participate in more positive or productive mindsets and activities, we can have a positive or productive influence. Similarly, as we experience the influences of others, we discover how their actions and reactions affect us and those around us. As we work further with the crown, we can learn to balance our own energy so that we remain in a state of balance even while others radiate dramatic fluctuations in their own energy.

When Sahasrara is in balance, we realize our connection to the universe and Divine power, and we gain a distinct sense of being part of the whole. We are not alone, and we are not stuck. We discover our will and our ability to tap into the infinite reservoir of energy the universe provides.

When in balance, you will discover that there is beauty in everything, even the things we might think of as gross or devastating. When you work closely with the crown, you begin to adjust your mundane perceptions and see how even the slimiest worm holds a valuable and beautiful purpose. In everything, there is balance and purpose. The crown chakra helps us work with this balance to find the beauty in everything.

Sahasrara brings you a higher level of consciousness, allowing your awareness to open and transcend. This does not mean a feeling of superiority. In fact, there is a level of humility that accompanies this level of understanding. Think of it like looking over a valley from a high vantage point, or climbing a flight of stairs to see more than you could previously. In fact, this is where the ego, or our need to feel superior to another, becomes mostly resolved. When we change our viewpoint, we begin to understand and take in information differently. We can process it without judgment or being critical. It has nothing to do with being superior to another.

Acting as the gateway between our physical consciousness and cosmic self, the crown chakra gives us the ability to connect with our higher self and intuition. Through this connection, we discover our divine ability and our inner wisdom. When you work with Sahasrara, you may find you understand obscure or complicated things a little easier. You may also find wisdom seems to flow through you when it previously would have been stunted or gone unnoticed.

SAHASRARA OUT OF BALANCE

When the crown chakra is blocked, overactive, or otherwise imbalanced, you feel it. It puts stress on your body and mind in various ways. On the physical level, we can experience exhaustion, skin disorders, extreme sensitivity to light, sound, heat, cold, etc. We may also experience weak or brittle bones and other skeletal issues.

On the mental level, you may feel scatter-brained or experience "mental fog." You may have trouble concentrating on tasks like reading or paying attention when someone is speaking. Apathy, lack of motivation, and lack of creativity are common signs of an imbalanced crown chakra. You may feel stuck, emotionally and spiritually. You may lack faith, inspiration, and have problems seeing the bigger picture. Additionally, you might experience difficulty with devotion and regular displays of devotion.

Much like the third eye chakra, the crown helps us focus and tap into our ability to perceive. When your crown chakra is neglected, it can affect your overall sense of self and well-being. You may discover a hindered ability to let go of material needs, or you may feel detached from the world around you. You most definitely will feel disconnected from the Divine. This detachment can lead to discontentment, bitterness, and resentment.

Another symptom of an imbalanced crown is finding yourself always looking to fill a void. You might feel like there is still something missing, yet you can't accurately pinpoint what this "something" is. You may find yourself trying to relieve this sensation through buying material things.

For a short time, you might feel that the void has been filled, only to lose this feeling as soon as the initial excitement or relief wears off. Sometimes an addiction can develop over time, as the fear of going without opens the void even further. Often, those who suffer from this imbalance buy and hoard items like shoes, clothes, food, and/or extra supplies they will never use. The result is having stockpiles of unused or expired items no one wants.

An imbalanced Sahasrara chakra can cause you to have a sense of elitism or superiority over others. Some disguise this through manipulation. Even some who claim to be "awake" or enlightened will use manipulative tactics to mask their imbalances. The important thing here to practice is self-awareness. If the need to feel superior over others overrides your ability to find peace and understanding, this chakra needs some attention and balancing.

Likewise, if you feel shame when you express or experience lower vibrational aspects of self (i.e., greed, rage, selfishness, etc.), it is time to become more aware of your mindsets and accept and balance your darker traits with your lighter ones. Being balanced does not mean you are somehow superhuman. It means you have learned to create a more authentic and even tone for expressing your whole self.

As always, when working with the seven-chakra system, it is essential to focus on all the chakras. Often it seems we spend the majority of our focus and time on the lower chakras when doing chakra work. Working with the upper chakras along with your lower chakras will help you balance the whole.

The beautiful thing about the crown chakra is that it seems to balance nicely almost on its own when all the other chakras have become more balanced. As I mentioned before, the upper chakras tend to work more closely with one another. Therefore, they have similar traits and abilities, allowing you to utilize common methods for establishing balance. This also means when you get one into a steady state of balance, the others may follow suit a little easier than expected.

When we begin working on all our chakras, we then start to realize how much they affect and balance one another. Through dedicated practice, your chakras can open up and heal as they begin to work with each other. Through this process of opening, you will be able to feel the release of any energetic constrictions from when they were working hard to compensate for one another.

HERBS FOR THE CROWN CHAKRA

Coconut, fennel, fenugreek, ginkgo biloba, gotu kola, mugwort, peppermint, tulsi, and white peony are all great plants to use when working with Sahasrara. You can also use florals like jasmine and rose.

Chocolate is also well known for helping humans feel good. Cacao, the raw ingredient of chocolate, has also been shown to improve cognitive function, which is the domain of the crown chakra. You can use cacao nibs and shells to make a delicious tea you can then blend with other flavors like cherry, coconut, and orange. You can also blend cacao into smoothies as a meal replacement or supplement.

EXERCISE FOR THE CROWN CHAKRA

In addition to the suggestions below, I recommend using the same exercise for the crown as you would for the third eye. These two chakras are very closely connected, and they seem to work closely together as a result.

Meditation. Spending time connecting to your higher self and your Divine guides is a great idea when working to balance and heal the crown. As noted in chapter 8, when we learn to create stillness in our minds and lives, we open ourselves to receiving. If you don't meditate regularly, try committing to five minutes every day for one week. The following week, go for seven minutes, and keep extending the time gradually from there until you get to at least 15 minutes per day. You will soon notice the difference between a day when you've meditated and a day when you haven't!

Mantras & Affirmations. Create mantras for yourself that help motivate you and guide you as you start your day. Focus them on creating energy and then balancing that energy. When we work with mantras or affirmations, we want to always make them in the present and positive tense. For the root chakra, "I am…" is the ideal way to begin a mantra. For the crown chakra, we want to start with "I know…" (See the mantra suggestions at the beginning of each chapter for starting points to inspire your own mantras.) Repeat your mantra to yourself several times throughout the day. Even if you don't feel the words to be "true" for you at the moment, acknowledge the positive energies of the words and appreciate yourself for doing this work.

Devotion. It is time to pay attention to your connection with the Divine power that protects and guides you. Create an altar where you leave daily offers of devotion. You can light a candle or some incense each morning before you wake up. Or in the evening before you go to bed, you can leave a flower or food offering to your Divine guardians and guides.

Chapter Ten: REIKI FOR BALANCING AND HEALING

As we seek to understand, heal, open, and balance our seven-chakra system, we should develop regular meditation and yoga practices for helping this process along. We should also get regular Reiki treatments, if at all possible. All of these practices are beneficial for the chakras, when utilized often and with intention, or a purpose-driven state of mind.

Like the concept of the chakra system itself, yoga and meditation are part of ancient Hindu vedic spirituality. Reiki is also believed to originate in India, but its modern form was not discovered and developed until the 19th century, in Japan.

The concept of energy centers in Japanese spiritual teachings differs somewhat from the chakras as we know them, but Reiki healing works seamlessly with the chakra system nonetheless, and the two are intertwined in many Western Reiki practices. This chapter will focus on Reiki as a highly impactful method for bringing your chakras into balance and yourself into general well-being, coming from my knowledge and experience as a Usui Reiki Master and Celtic Reiki Master.

Reiki is a form of energy healing. The Japanese word "reiki" combines the words for "soul" or "spirit" (*rei*) and "vital energy" (*ki*), and is often translated as "universal life energy." As practitioners, we recognize the healing energy of Reiki as an infinite and intelligent life force. Most see it as cosmic energy flowing through the practitioner from somewhere in the universe.

It is widely agreed that this makes the healer (the Reiki practitioner) a conduit, not the source, of the healing act or energy. The Reiki practitioner is connected to or opened to this flow of Reiki energy through a series of Reiki attunements. An attunement is a ritual in which adjustments are made to the Reiki student's subtle energy body by a Reiki master. This process allows the student's body to become a channel for Reiki energy.

Reiki energy flows through the individual and is led through a series of hand movements and positions, or specific symbols. The energy guides the practitioner to the areas of the body that need attention.

Essentially, all the practitioner needs to do is allow the energy to flow and move in the general direction of where the energy needs to go. But in order to do this, the practitioner is tasked with gaining and utilizing the skills of sensing, listening for, and recognizing the subtleties of the energy. As practitioners takes direction from the energy flowing through them, they must have gained the ability to recognize the route the energy must take. This route may vary with each individual, and even over the course of several sessions with the same individual.

There are many forms of Reiki out there available to you for your health and well-being. From its origins (Usui Reiki) to Violet Flame, Dragon, Crystal Reiki, and Celtic Reiki, we have a variety of modalities we can utilize to meet our needs. Each Reiki style or pattern will have its own particular healing philosophy used by the practitioner or master. Each form will also have its own degree system. This is how we develop the concept of *practice*. After all, if you have nothing to practice, you have no modality.

Mikao Usui is credited with rediscovering the root energy healing system, which is now known as Reiki. Master Usui is the founder of the first Reiki system called Usui Reiki, which has been passed through several Reiki Masters to today's Usui Reiki Masters. Currently, Usui Reiki is the most widely used form of Reiki practice. Usui has many levels when seeking help in healing and balancing the chakra system.

First Degree or Level I Reiki

The first degree connects the individual to the energy of Reiki. It opens the energy channel and permits the student to channel Reiki energy for personal use. This level is open to anyone. No previous experience or preparation is required. You only need an attunement to become open and begin using Reiki energy on yourself. Some also believe that at this level, you can use Reiki energy to help heal small animals and pets.

Second Degree or Level II Reiki

At this stage, the practitioner is opened up to a great understanding of Reiki energy. This is also where the student is given power symbols to use. At this level, the practitioner can begin offering Reiki healing to others, including plants and animals.

Third Degree or Level III Reiki

Level three is where you gain some level of mastery. You are now able to attune others to Reiki energy as you receive your master symbol for use in your practice. You also learn to combine the Reiki symbols to generate more profound and more effective healing during your sessions. You can perform healing on yourself, others, animals, plants, and the earth.

Reiki Master

The Reiki Master has gone through all three levels and is now qualified to teach the degrees to others as well as provide healing treatments and attunements.

DISTANCE REIKI

Distance Reiki is widely practiced today. While distance healing has gained a lot of acceptance, distance Reiki attunements are more controversial. Many practitioners believe that an individual can only receive an attunement through physical contact or interaction, meaning the master or practitioner must be in the same location as the person they treat or attune. Personally, I don't see this being necessary. Here are my thoughts:

Energy, and especially cosmic energy, is boundless, having no limitations regarding time and space. In my experience, using this as the standard belief or understanding, distance or remote sessions and attunements are effective. If, as Reiki practitioners, we genuinely believe that the energy we direct is expansive, intelligent, and infinite, then why couldn't it have the ability to move beyond our preconceived ideas or boundaries?

As humans, we often have a limited view of what is possible. After all, we can only understand and perceive what we can recognize. Anything beyond this is impossible or fictional.

As an energy healer, I challenge this limited view of energy and the universe, because universal energy defies our limited understandings. Even in science, what was once thought to be fact is challenged each day as new discoveries are made. This challenges our perspective and boundaries of what is possible, opening us up to new possibilities. Therefore in my practice, I believe in the ability of Reiki to be more than we think and perceive.

To appreciate this, let us examine the Reiki framework with a broader lens. Reiki (or any 'universal' force) exists at every point of the universe. In fact, the energy we use in Reiki is the energy of the universe. Because we live within the universe, we are also part of the universe. This allows the energy of the universe to flow through us if we allow it.

The training one goes through to become a Reiki practitioner teaches the individual how to enable this energy to flow. But it does not stop there. This training also teaches the practitioner how to communicate with this energy. As I mentioned before, the Reiki practitioner must learn how to read the energy so it can be directed to the right areas or locations. This ability or learned skill of indirect communication allows Reiki to work in the space where it is most needed.

The challenge is this: humans are physical. Due to our physicality, we tend to favor the physical world along with the physical cues generated using physical means. This is also why most of us tend to focus most on the lower three chakras.

When we are overly connected to the material with our mindsets, social conditioning, and so on, we will find it very difficult to shift our consciousness to accept and become aware of the nonphysical world. When we glimpse the nonphysical, either by accident or through a willful introduction, we can find ourselves developing a habit of creating rationality around the experience. We explain things away when we cannot fully accept or understand the lesson.

For example, a woman seeks out a Reiki treatment out of need and curiosity. She has been working with her doctor to relieve the arthritis pain in her right knee. Nothing has successfully worked for her so far. At this point, she will try anything.

After her first Reiki treatment, she notices something different—her pain has lessened. But because she has been told and taught that relief can only come from a medical doctor under the Western medical model, she has a hard time believing that the Reiki treatment was genuinely effective. But to satisfy her curiosity, she returns the next week for her next treatment.

After additional treatments, she feels even better. Her range of motion seems to be improved, and the pain is lessened. Still, she has a hard time believing that "woo-woo" energy healing could have this kind of benefit. She thinks to herself that it must be a fluke and that the treatments her doctor has prescribed must finally be working.

In this state of constant denial, we see how powerful conditioning and social programming can be. Even when we see the benefits and positive results from another method, we can explain it away. Eventually, we will convince ourselves that the perceived benefit was all in our heads.

The problem with this is that how we view unlimited potential is how we receive potential. The client must be open and willing to receive healing if healing is to occur. If we convince ourselves that we are limited and that there are no possibilities, we will have blocked potential and receive a limited benefit. Unlimited potential offers us focus, strength, tangibility, physicality, and comprehension. Whereas placing limits on energy and what we believe it can do depletes the possibility, even when we desperately need the benefit.

Reiki practitioners and masters have been trained to open themselves up to these unlimited possibilities, allowing their understanding to grow over time. In the beginning, Usui Reiki brought to us an initial understanding of universal energy and how it can work through human beings. In newer modalities, such as Celtic Reiki, the practice encompasses all of the same methods as Usui Reiki, but expands to further incorporate the energy of trees, the stars, plants/herbs, the elements, and a whole range of other universal aspects.

The Celts and other indigenous people were enveloped in their environment, the earth and all living creatures upon it were sacred. We live in very different times, yet we can still make use of the world and resources around us. So when we seek to heal our energy centers using thought, practice, and energy, we need to recognize the expansiveness of the energy we use. We should be open to the unlimited potential the universe has to create and maintain. The only limitations out there are the ones we place on ourselves.

CONCLUSION

Working through the seven chakras, we can see how each plays a vital role in our emotional, spiritual, physical, and mental well-being. As we dig deeper into our needs, imbalances, and abilities, we quickly learn that humans are complicated creatures. But we have a tremendous power to heal and restore our energy on many levels.

Practices like yoga, meditation, Reiki, and more help us recover our energy and vitality when we need it most. Creating a daily practice where we pay attention to our energy centers and physical, emotional, and spiritual needs will help us create and maintain a sense of wellness and balance as a whole. Using plants, movement, and adjusting our mindset only further supports our efforts.

The ideas, knowledge, and experiences shared in this book are far from complete. There is much to explore when it comes to the chakras. I hope you found this book helpful to you as you move forward with your wellness. I hope you are inspired to know more as you work your way to wellness and understanding.

SUGGESTIONS FOR FURTHER READING

Most of this knowledge comes from my training as a Reiki Master, but there are several books and resources I have used on my own journey. Here are a few to start with in your own explorations:

Chakra Healing: A Beginner's Guide to Self-Healing Techniques that Balance the Chakras. Margarita Alcantra, 2017.

Awakening Kundalini: The Path to Radical Freedom. Lawrence Edwards, 2012.

Chakra Balancing Made Simple and Easy (2nd Edition). Michael Hetherington, 2012.

The Effect of Diaphragmatic Breathing on Attention, Negative Affect and Stress in Healthy Adults (Frontiers in Psychology). Xiao Ma, et al., 2017.

Breathing: The Master Key to Self Healing. Andrew Weil, 2001.

Chakras For Beginners - How to Awaken And Balance Chakras, Radiate Positive Energy And Heal Yourself. Michael Williams, 2016.

ABOUT THE AUTHORS

Leandra Witchwood is a Modern Witch living in South-Central Pennsylvania and owns The Witchwood Teahouse, where she hand-blends loose-leaf teas for ritual, spell work, everyday enjoyment, and wellness. Leandra is the author of four books: *Magick in the Kitchen*, *Witchcraft for Beginners*, *13 Essential Spells*, and *From the Witch's Shadow*. She is the Elder Priestess of her coven, Indigo Hearth, where she oversees and teaches her specific style of Eclectic Witchcraft, incorporating elements of Magickal Herbalism, Kitchen Witchery, folk magick, and more. Leandra's education and experience draw from traditional, ceremonial, and modern Witchcraft. She holds various certificates, including Shadow Work Mastery, Usui Reiki Master, Celtic Reiki Master, NPL, EFT, and Divine Feminine Studies. She runs a coaching practice offering Dark Mirror coaching for witches interested in Shadow Work and spiritual direction sessions for those seeking clarity on their path. Learn more at **LeandraWitchwood.com.**

Lisa Chamberlain is the successful author of more than twenty books on Wicca, divination, and magical living, including *Green Witchcraft for Beginners*, *Wicca Book of Herbal Spells*, *Elemental Magic*, *Magic and the Law of Attraction*, *Runes for Beginners,* and *Tarot for Beginners.* An intuitive empath, she has been exploring witchcraft, magic, and other esoteric paths since her teenage years. Her spiritual journey has included a traditional solitary Wiccan practice as well as more eclectic studies across a wide range of belief systems. Lisa's focus is on positive magic that promotes self-empowerment for the good of the whole. You can find out more about her and her work at her website, **wiccaliving.com.**

THREE FREE AUDIOBOOKS PROMOTION

Don't forget, you can now enjoy **three audiobooks completely free of charge** when you start a free 30-day trial with Audible.

If you're new to the Craft, *Wicca Starter Kit* contains three of Lisa's most popular books for beginning Wiccans. You can download it for free at:

www.wiccaliving.com/free-wiccan-audiobooks

Or, if you're wanting to expand your magical skills, check out *Spellbook Starter Kit,* with three collections of spellwork featuring the powerful energies of candles, colors, crystals, mineral stones, and magical herbs. Download over 150 spells for free at:

www.wiccaliving.com/free-spell-audiobooks

Members receive free audiobooks every month, as well as exclusive discounts. And, if you don't want to continue with Audible, just remember to cancel your membership. You won't be charged a cent, and you'll get to keep your books!

Happy listening!

MORE BOOKS BY LISA CHAMBERLAIN

Wicca for Beginners: A Guide to Wiccan Beliefs, Rituals, Magic, and Witchcraft

Wicca Book of Spells: A Book of Shadows for Wiccans, Witches, and Other Practitioners of Magic

Wicca Herbal Magic: A Beginner's Guide to Practicing Wiccan Herbal Magic, with Simple Herb Spells

Wicca Book of Herbal Spells: A Book of Shadows for Wiccans, Witches, and Other Practitioners of Herbal Magic

Wicca Candle Magic: A Beginner's Guide to Practicing Wiccan Candle Magic, with Simple Candle Spells

Wicca Book of Candle Spells: A Book of Shadows for Wiccans, Witches, and Other Practitioners of Candle Magic

Wicca Crystal Magic: A Beginner's Guide to Practicing Wiccan Crystal Magic, with Simple Crystal Spells

Wicca Book of Crystal Spells: A Book of Shadows for Wiccans, Witches, and Other Practitioners of Crystal Magic

Tarot for Beginners: A Guide to Psychic Tarot Reading, Real Tarot Card Meanings, and Simple Tarot Spreads

Runes for Beginners: A Guide to Reading Runes in Divination, Rune Magic, and the Meaning of the Elder Futhark Runes

Wicca Moon Magic: A Wiccan's Guide and Grimoire for Working Magic with Lunar Energies

Wicca Wheel of the Year Magic: A Beginner's Guide to the Sabbats, with History, Symbolism, Celebration Ideas, and Dedicated Sabbat Spells

Wicca Kitchen Witchery: A Beginner's Guide to Magical Cooking, with Simple Spells and Recipes

Wicca Essential Oils Magic: A Beginner's Guide to Working with Magical Oils, with Simple Recipes and Spells

Wicca Elemental Magic: A Guide to the Elements, Witchcraft, and Magical Spells

Wicca Magical Deities: A Guide to the Wiccan God and Goddess, and Choosing a Deity to Work Magic With

Wicca Living a Magical Life: A Guide to Initiation and Navigating Your Journey in the Craft

Magic and the Law of Attraction: A Witch's Guide to the Magic of Intention, Raising Your Frequency, and Building Your Reality

Wicca Altar and Tools: A Beginner's Guide to Wiccan Altars, Tools for Spellwork, and Casting the Circle

Wicca Finding Your Path: A Beginner's Guide to Wiccan Traditions, Solitary Practitioners, Eclectic Witches, Covens, and Circles

Wicca Book of Shadows: A Beginner's Guide to Keeping Your Own Book of Shadows and the History of Grimoires

Modern Witchcraft and Magic for Beginners: A Guide to Traditional and Contemporary Paths, with Magical Techniques for the Beginner Witch

FREE GIFT REMINDER

Just a reminder that Lisa is giving away an exclusive, free spell book as a thank-you gift to new readers!

Little Book of Spells contains ten spells that are ideal for newcomers to the practice of magic, but are also suitable for any level of experience.

Read it on read on your laptop, phone, tablet, Kindle or Nook device by visiting:

www.wiccaliving.com/bonus

DID YOU ENJOY *CHAKRAS FOR WITCHES*?

Thanks so much for reading this book! I know there are many great books out there about Wicca, so I really appreciate you choosing this one.

If you enjoyed the book, I have a small favor to ask—would you take a couple of minutes to leave a review for this book on Amazon?

Your feedback will help me to make improvements to this book, and to create even better ones in the future. It will also help me develop new ideas for books on other topics that might be of interest to you. Thanks in advance for your help!